PENELOPE ROSKELL'S COMPLETE PIANIST SERIES

Essential Piano Technique

LEVEL 3

Early intermediate

by
Penelope Roskell

Original music by Aaron Burrows

ALLE RECHTE VORBEHALTEN · ALL RIGHTS RESERVED
EDITION PETERS
PUBLISHED BY FABER MUSIC
Leipzig · London · New York

For Richard Griffiths

Author acknowledgements

These books would not have been possible without the support of many friends and colleagues. In particular I would like to thank:

Huei Flowers, Inês Costa, Garreth Brooke, Monika Walo, Clare Spencer and Christine Dunford, Richard Dinsmore, Gwen Harborne, Dr Oliver Griffiths and members of the Roskell Academy.

This edition © 2025 by Faber Music Ltd
Brownlow Yard, 12 Roger Street, London WC1N 2JU
Cover portrait of Penelope Roskell by kind permission of John Batten
Page design by Liz Ogden
Illustrations by Eilidh Muldoon and Liz Ogden
Music setting by John Rogers
Video production by Informance
Printed in England by Caligraving Ltd
All rights reserved

ISMN 979-0-57702-488-2

Contents

	Introduction		4
	Warm-up routine		5
Agility and shaping	Tumbling fingers	*Tango*	6
	Elegant endings	*Theme* (Gurlitt)	9
Chords	Large parachutes	*Midnight Blue*	11
	Large jellyfish jumps	*Little Waltz*	14
Accents	Accents – jump LAND		16
	Accented syncopation	*Polka* (Glinka); *Charleston*	17
Scales	Starting on a black note	*Czerny-esque*	19
	Melodic minor scales	*Elegy*	21
Upbeats	Upbeats	*Children at Play* (Bartók)	24
	Run-ups	*Piper's Tune*	26
	Revising techniques	*Zingarese* (Haydn)	29
Arpeggios	Two-octave arpeggios (left hand)		30
	Left-hand arpeggio groups		31
	Two-octave arpeggios (right hand)	*Harpist's Serenade*	32
Exploring sound	Dynamics explorer	*Cosmic Bells*	35
	Pianissimo cantabile	*Valse*	37
	Melody and accompaniment	*Melody* (Schumann)	39
	Left-hand melodies	*Night Journey* (Gurlitt)	41
Leaps	Wide leaps	*Prelude* (Tetsel)	43
Repetition	Duplets and triplets	*Triplets in Lydian Mode* (Bartók)	45
	Repeated notes	*Play It Again*	47
	Repeated chords	*The New Doll* (Tchaikovsky);	50
		Celebration Dance	52
	Combining techniques	*Fanfare Minuet* (Duncombe)	53
Ornaments	Mordents	*Grandmother's Minuet* (Grieg)	54
	Trills	*The Trickster*	56
	Inverted mordents	*Menuet in D Minor* (de la Guerre)	58
Two voices in one hand	Relaxed hand and fingers		59
	Held notes	*I Danced With a Pig* (Bartók)	61
	Resting thumb		63
	Legato thirds	*Thirds Against a Single Voice* (Bartók)	64
Pedalling	Direct pedalling	*Sad at Heart* (Fuchs)	66
		Hat Tip Polka	68
	Teaching notes		74

Introduction

Welcome to Level 3!

This book will guide you progressively from elementary level through to early intermediate level. You will study many new techniques which will give you a solid foundation in healthy piano playing and help you progress quickly and enjoyably. You will also learn how to play many beautiful new pieces expressively and with artistry.

If you are new to this series, you may find it helpful to look at the Revision suggestions in the Teaching notes at the back of the book which direct you to related exercises in other books in the series.

The Practice pointers and Technique tips will remind you of the most important points to remember when practising. To explore techniques further, do also check out the extension activities ⟫ and the recommended pieces which have been carefully chosen for you.

To the teacher

This is the fifth book in the *Essential Piano Technique* series. It develops some of the techniques studied in the previous books, as well as introducing many new techniques. On completing the book, students will have progressed from around Grade 2 (elementary) to Grade 4 (early intermediate) level confidently and with ease.

Technique is all taught within a musical context. Each technique is introduced initially as a simple exercise away from the piano, followed by an exercise at the piano and a musical piece which focuses on that particular technique.

Students who are new to this series will benefit from revising some of the fundamental techniques from previous books in the *Essential Piano Technique* series, especially **Rainbows**, the **Parachute touch**, **Down-ups**, **Jellyfish jumps**, the **Skipping-rope** technique and **Legato pedalling**.

The progression has been planned very carefully to guide your student successfully through all the challenges encountered at this level. However, you can dip in and out of chapters as and when the need arises for particular students.

Explanations of the learning objectives, more detailed teaching tips and further suggestions for related pieces are available in the Teaching Notes at the back of the book. These Teaching Notes can be supplemented by accessing the Roskell Academy website (www.roskellacademy.com) which offers teachers supporting material and access to training and certification in the Roskell method. You can also find more information about each aspect of technique in *The Complete Pianist: from healthy technique to natural artistry* (Edition Peters, 2020).

 Video demonstrations can be accessed via the QR code, or by visiting www.fabermusic.com/ep/essential-piano-technique

Warm-up routine

Warming up before playing will help you begin your practice with relaxed arms and hands. You can do all these standing up.

Windmills

Swing your arms in a big circle like a windmill. Swing each arm separately, then together.

Empty sleeves

Twist your body from side to side, letting your arms swing loosely around your body.

Ready to play

Breathe in and lift your arms above the keyboard, then breathe out and let your hands sink down to rest on the keys, ready to play.

Monkey

Lean your body forwards a little and swing both arms from side to side like a monkey!

Deep breathing

Take several deep breaths in and out.

Shoulder shrugs

Breathe in as you raise your shoulders. Breathe out as you drop your shoulders back down. Repeat five times, feeling your arms hanging loosely.

Shoulder rolls

Place your right hand lightly on your right shoulder and your left hand on your left shoulder. Draw big circles with your elbows. Breathe in as your elbows float up; breathe out as they float down.

Tumbling fingers

Here you will learn to play quickly, in semiquavers (sixteenth notes).

♩ = ♫ = ♬

crotchet (quarter note) = quavers (eighth notes) = semiquavers (sixteenth notes)

Have you ever typed on an old-fashioned typewriter? It's hard work! It's easier to play ♬ when your fingers play lightly, as if you are tapping on a laptop.

Cloud hands

Imagine your hands are clouds floating in the air, then twiddle your fingers lightly, like rain drizzling down.

Wavy arms

Draw some big waves in the air in front of you, then draw smaller scoops with the right hand, then the left hand, then hands together.

Twiddle your fingers as you draw each wave.

The parachute
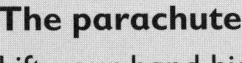
Lift your hand high above your head and imagine it is dangling from a parachute. Then let it float down to rest lightly upon a flat surface, such as a table or the closed keyboard lid. Repeat this parachute movement at the piano, landing lightly on your fifth finger. Do it several times, gradually making the movement smaller until it just feels as though your wrist is 'breathing'.

Keep your arm light, like a floating parachute, as you play the next exercises.

The Mexican wave

On a flat surface such as a table, let your fingers tumble down one after the other as if you're twiddling your fingers.

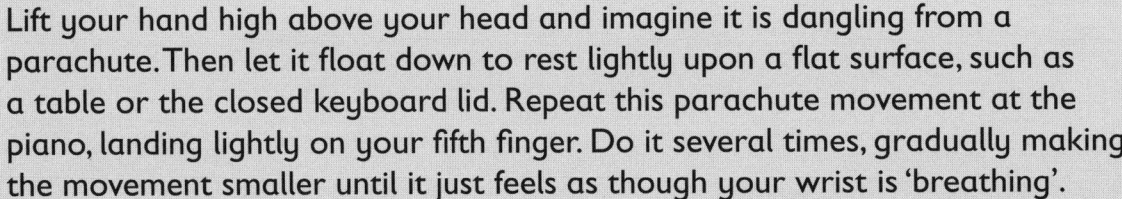

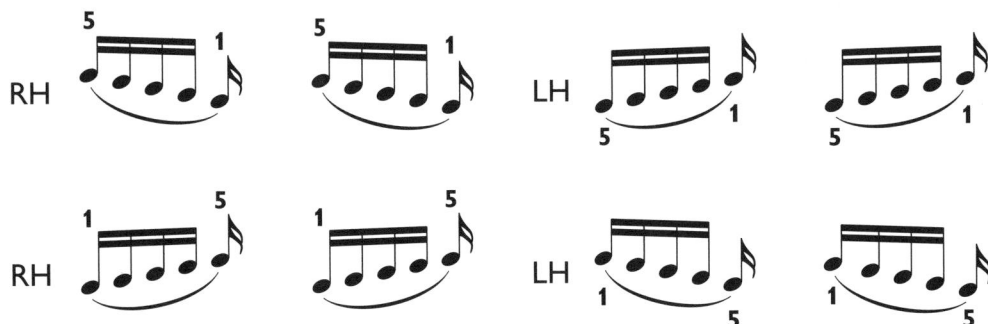

Now practise **Mexican waves** at the piano. Parachute onto the first note of each phrase, then let your fingers tumble quickly onto the keys, one after the other.

Feel your wrist 'breathing' up and down in the rest between each slur.

Tumbling up

Look at the following pattern then play it without the music. Feel your arms floating gracefully over the keyboard as they move between hand positions.

Tumbling down

 Technique Tips
- ✔ In **Tango** on page 8, parachute down onto the first note of each slur.
- ✔ Play with tumbling fingers and float off elegantly at the end of each phrase.

 Now transpose this exercise into D minor, A minor, and E major, ready for the next piece.

7

Tango

Tango, steady but incisive

Aaron Burrows

Elegant endings

Pianists often forget to listen to the ends of notes! Some phrases, including those in **Tumbling fingers**, need to end elegantly.

Floating wrists
Rest your hand on a table. Let your wrist float upwards gradually until your fingers are lifted from the table.

Floating off

At the piano, let your wrist float up as it gradually lifts each finger off the note.

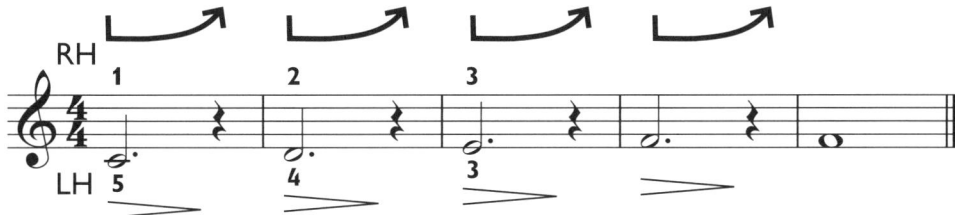

Listen to the smooth ending of each note and the atmospheric silence in the rests.

Graceful slurs

Lift your wrist during each slur and float off the last note very gently. Listen to the *diminuendo*.

Chord endings

Now play these chords, lifting your hand very smoothly for a gradual ending.

Theme

This piece is taken from a *Theme and Variation* by Cornelius Gurlitt. The chords are marked with a slur and a *staccato*. This means that you need to lift your hand smoothly away from the keyboard after each chord.

Cornelius Gurlitt
arr. Penelope Roskell

Lift your hand especially slowly from the last chord so that it dies away very gradually and creates a magical atmosphere.

Look carefully at the length of the notes in another piece you have learnt. Will you end the notes abruptly or gradually?

Large parachutes

How big an interval can you reach when you open your hand to full stretch? Pieces at this level often include chords with bigger intervals (gaps between notes). You need to know how to play these comfortably.

Fan hands

Open and close your hands like a fan. Then stretch your hands above your head, spreading your fingers out wide. Feel the palms of your hands opening. Relax your hands then spread them out wide again. Stretch your hands out to your side, spread your fingers wide then relax them.

Pot of gold

Draw a big rainbow in the air in front of you and pretend you are dropping some gold at each end. Try dropping a heavy pot, then a light coin.

Dropping gold

Now use the rainbow movement to drop onto some open fifths (for example D and A) at the piano. Remember to relax your hand as you float between the fifths.

The splay

When playing bigger intervals such as sixths or sevenths, you need to open out your hand to reach the notes but keep both your hand and wrist as relaxed as possible.

Repeat the rainbow movement but imagine you are dropping a *big* pot of gold!

Play this exercise slowly, letting your hand relax and close back to its normal shape during each rest.

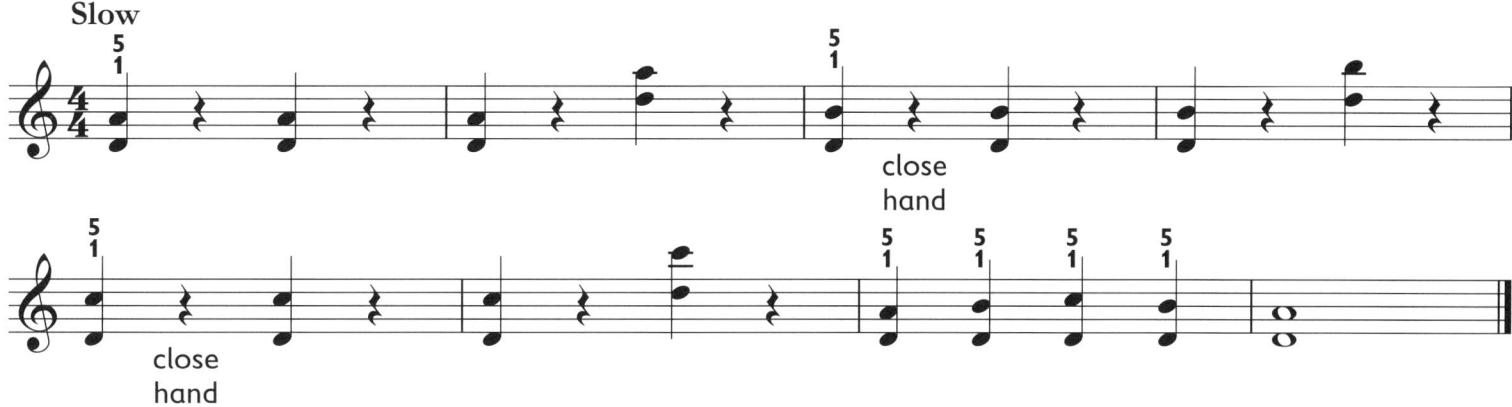

11

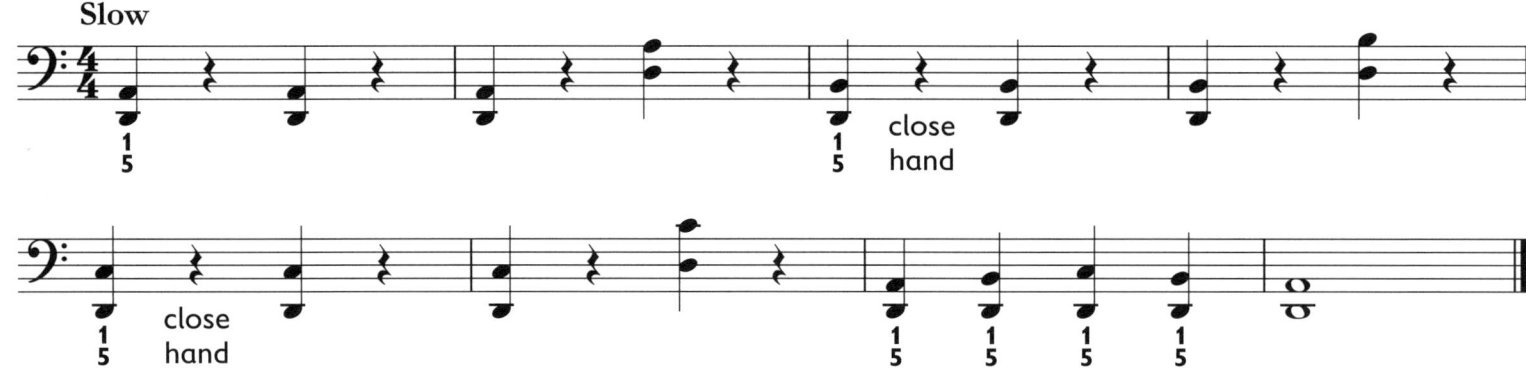

Technique Tips

- ✔ Drop your wrist slightly as you parachute onto each chord.
- ✔ Remember to relax your hand during the rest.
- ✔ Look at the notes you are moving towards, so your hand moves without hesitating.
- ✔ Keep your arm moving in one flowing rainbow motion – don't stop and start.

 Play some triads, relaxing your hand between the chords. You can add some dynamic contrast to these exercises by dropping your hand heavily like an elephant or lightly like an insect.

Seventh chords

In this exercise, imagine your hand is parachuting very smoothly down onto each chord. Remember to relax your hand fully as it floats back up during the rests.

Large jellyfish jumps

Jellyfish jumps will help you play wider intervals *staccato*.

Swimming jellyfish
Move your hand around in the air like a small pulsating jellyfish swimming in the ocean. Feel your hand relax like jelly each time it floats upwards. Now imagine your hand is a bigger jellyfish – open it a little further as you swim down, then close your hand as it floats up.

Large jellyfish jumps

Play some *staccato* fifths on the piano, feeling your hand relax between each interval. Then extend your hand to play a sixth, a seventh and, if your hand is big enough, an octave.

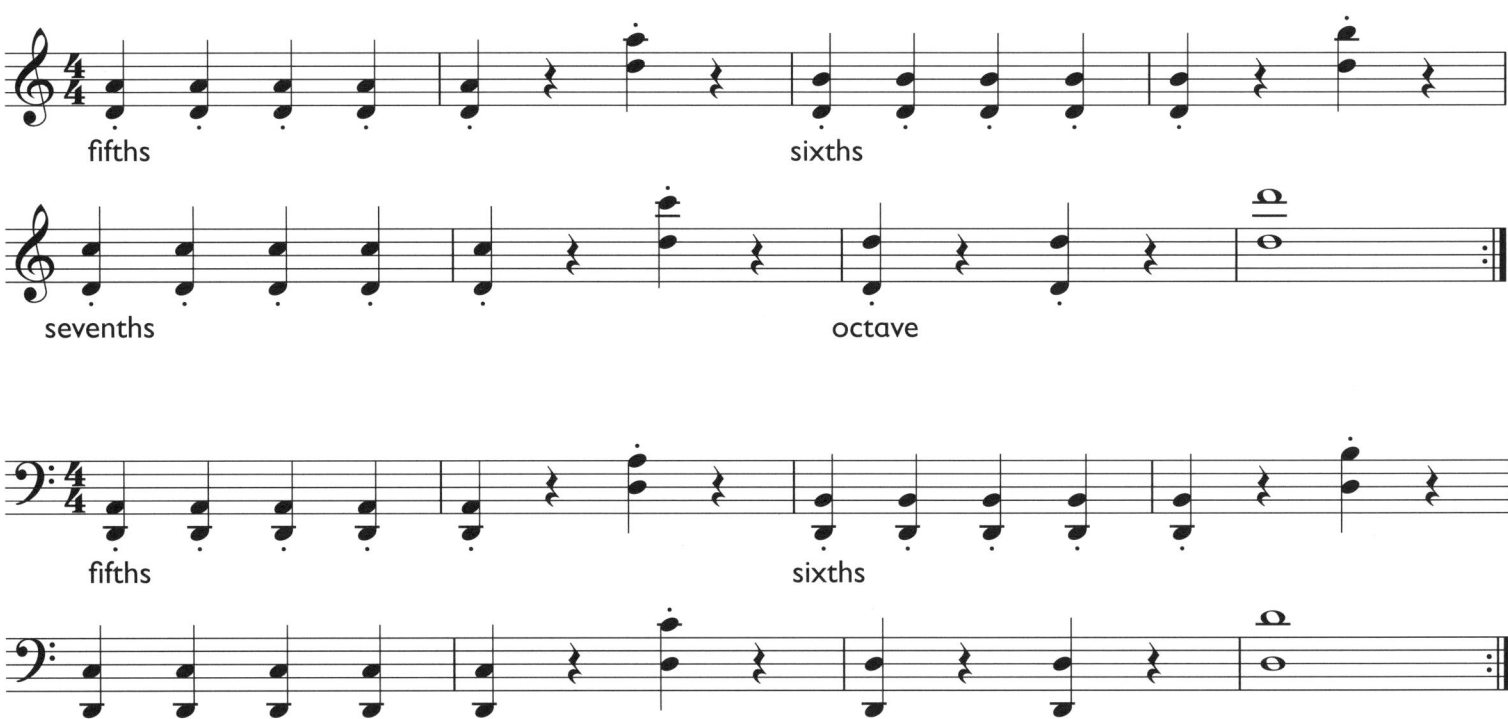

Now practise these hands together.

Technique Tips
- ✔ Practise slowly at first, lifting your hand quite high between the chords. Then play a little faster, keeping your hand closer to the keys.
- ✘ If you can't quite stretch the whole octave in the final bars, just play the top D!

 Also use **Jellyfish jumps** to play the seventh chords on page 12 staccato.

Little Waltz

Use **Jellyfish jumps** for all the intervals in this piece.

You may also like:
Walter Carroll: 'Under the Cherry Tree' from *Forest Fantasies*
Carl Czerny: 'Etude in Sixths' Op. 139 No. 7

Accents – jump LAND

A note written with an accent is played more loudly than its neighbours. Accents help to add excitement and expression to our playing.

Accents are usually written like this:

Here you will learn to create an accent by dropping your hand from a greater height.

Jump LAND

Spring lightly off the *staccato* upbeat then drop firmly to create the accent on the second note. You may find it helps to jump quite high at first:

Hop and LAND

Energetic accents can also be written like this:

Technique Tips
- ✔ Remember to drop onto accented notes.
- ✘ Don't push down!

You may also like:

Dmitry Kabalevsky: 'Funny Event' Op. 39 No. 7

Pam Wedgwood: 'Break-out' from *Up-Grade! Piano Grades 2–3*

Accented syncopation

When an accent occurs on a weak beat it is called syncopation. You can use the 'jump LAND' technique to play the syncopation.

Polka

In this Polka by Glinka, **jump** off the first beat of the bar to **LAND** firmly on the accent on the second beat. Look at the fingering in this piece. The thumb plays all the accents, which helps them sound heavy.

Mikhail Glinka
arr. Penelope Roskell

Listening challenge:
- Check that the right-hand accents are held and the left-hand *staccato* is bouncy!

You may also like:

Lajos Papp: 'Shepherd's Dance' from *22 Little Piano Pieces*
Mikhail Glinka: 'Polka' (complete version)
Robert Schumann: 'Wild Rider' Op. 68 No. 8

Charleston

The *tenuto* marking (—) is a softer kind of accent. Do a **Jellyfish jump** on the *staccato*, then land gently but firmly on the *tenuto* chord.

Aaron Burrows

18

Starting on a black note

Not all scales start on a white note. Here you will learn some scales that start on a black note.

B♭ major hand position

Let's revise the B♭ major hand position you learnt in Level 2. Remember, you can help your fingers play the black notes comfortably by moving your hand forward a little and slotting your other fingers between the black notes.

B♭ major scale

However, if you play the complete B♭ scale starting with the thumb, it feels wrong as your thumb needs to turn under:

Technique Tips

Here are some useful principles for fingering these scales:

✔ The thumb plays a white note.
✔ The third and fourth fingers play black notes.

Practise the B♭ major scale hands separately in one octave then two, starting on the third finger. Then play hands together, adding one note at a time.

E♭ major scale

The E♭ major scale also starts with the third finger. It's a great scale to play hands together in contrary motion, as the fingering is the same in both hands.

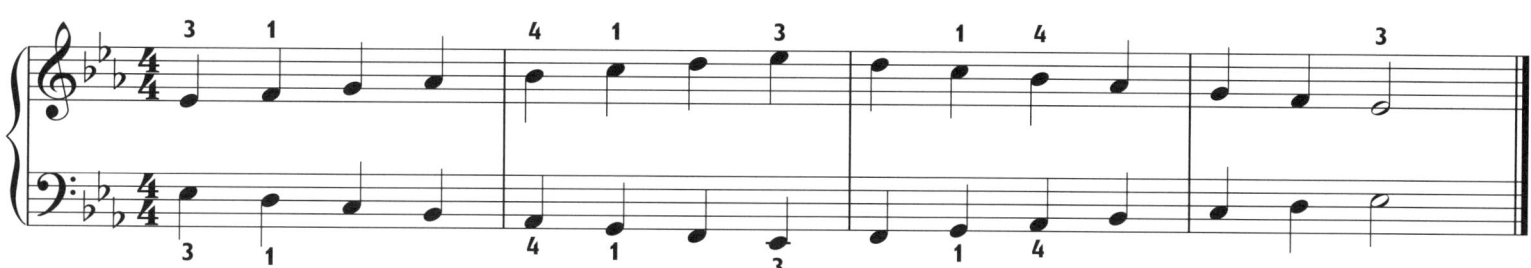

Skipping rope

You can use the **Skipping-rope** technique to help the thumb swing easily under the black note. Let your arm hang loosely from your shoulder like a skipping rope, so your thumb can swing easily to its note.

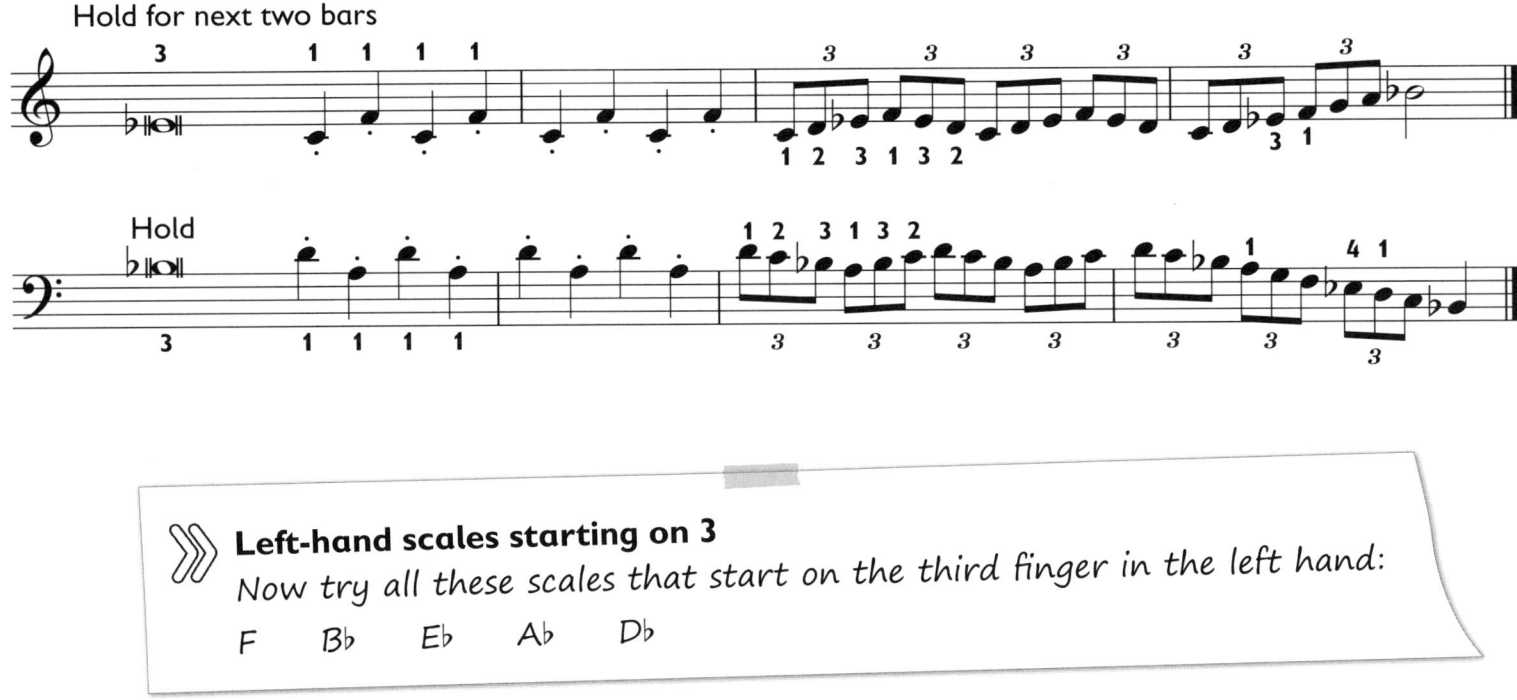

> **Left-hand scales starting on 3**
> Now try all these scales that start on the third finger in the left hand:
> F   Bb   Eb   Ab   Db

Czerny-esque

Play your part hands separately first, one octave higher than written. Then play hands together one octave apart, while your teacher plays the accompaniment.

Aaron Burrows

Melodic minor scales

Here you will learn about melodic minor scales – the notes are slightly different for the ascending and descending scale.

Ascending scale: the sixth and seventh notes are raised.

Descending scale: the scale reverts to the natural minor.

A melodic minor

Practise the A melodic minor scale until you get used to how it *sounds* and *feels* under your hand. You could try to play it with your eyes closed. Then play the two-octave scale in each hand.

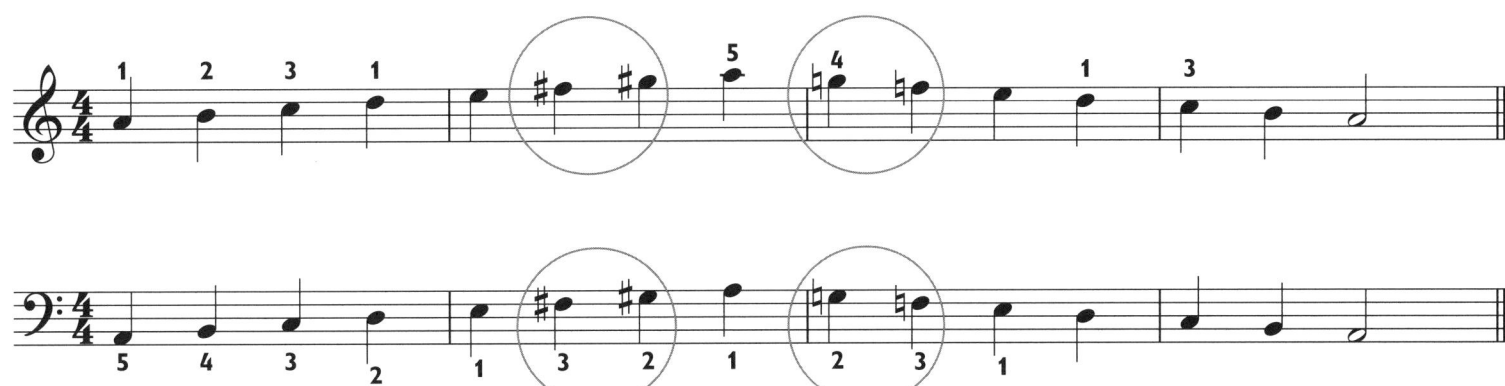

Before you start:
- Look at the pattern of black and white notes on the piano.
- Mime the fingering on your lap before you touch the piano.
- Position your hand so you can reach the black notes easily.

D melodic minor

You will now find it easy to learn other melodic minor scales:

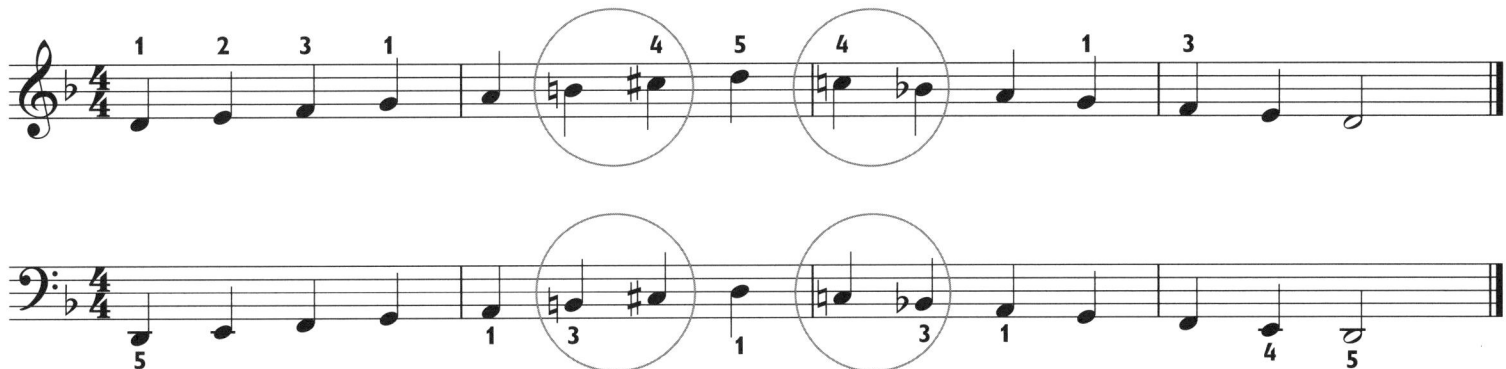

Also extend the D minor scale to two octaves.

G melodic minor

Look carefully at the fingering for G minor and notice that the third and fourth fingers play the black notes.

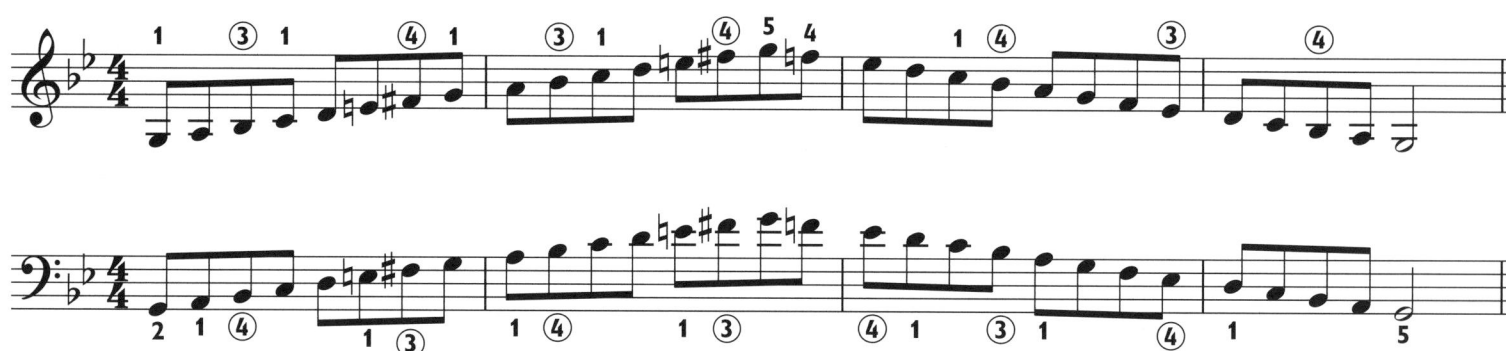

You can practise this scale using the **Add-a-note** technique:

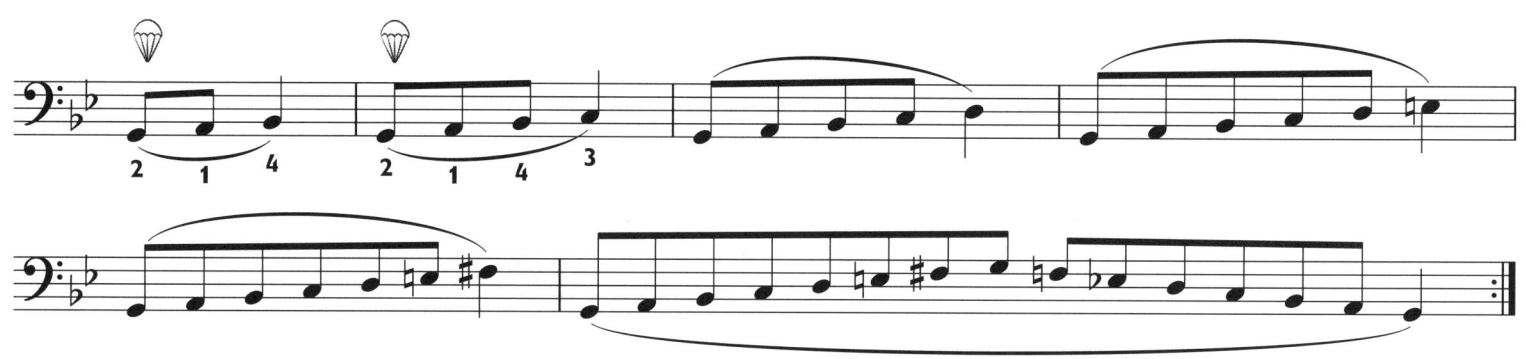

Technique Tips
- ✔ Parachute onto the first note.
- ✔ Play smoothly and expressively, using a stroking arm movement.
- ✔ Listen carefully and check that the fourth finger plays as firmly as the others.

Now practise each hand separately until they develop *muscle memory* (your fingers start to remember where to go!).

》 Can you work out the notes for the C melodic minor scale?

Revise the harmonic minor scales of A, D, G and C minor and compare them with the melodic minor scale.

Look out for snippets of melodic minor scales in your pieces and remember to play them expressively.

You might also like:

Diane Hidy: 'White Key Minors' from *Smart Scales*

Cornelius Gurlitt: Study in A minor Op. 82 No. 52

Elegy

Andante

Aaron Burrows

You may also like:

Cornelius Gurlitt: 'The Hardy Horseman' Op. 117 No. 32

Allan Bullard: 'Scalic Scherzo' from *Mastering the Piano Level 3 (Lang Lang)*

Upbeats

The first beat of the bar is known as the main beat. The note before the main beat is the upbeat. It sounds more interesting if the upbeat is played more quietly than the main beat.

And ONE!
Clap this rhythm. Say ONE loudly and clap boldly on each main beat. Clap the upbeat (the 'and') more quietly.

and ONE   and ONE   and ONE   and ONE

Down UP!
Say 'down' as you parachute your hand softly down onto your leg. Then push your wrist quickly up and away from you as you say 'UP'! Feel your fingertips press down into your leg energetically as your wrist springs up.

Repeat several times, saying:

down UP! down UP! down UP! down UP!

Now place a small toy on the back of your hand. Flick the toy away from you as your hand springs up! How far can you flick the toy?

Spring-offs

Play D with a low wrist. Then flick your wrist up as your third finger plays the main beat firmly.

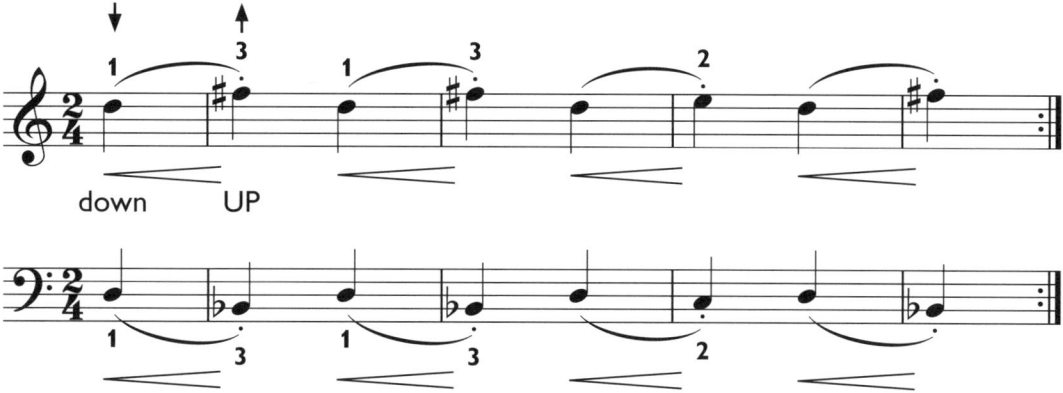

down   UP

We have lift-off

Spring off the last note of each slur, following the wrist movement shown by the arrows.

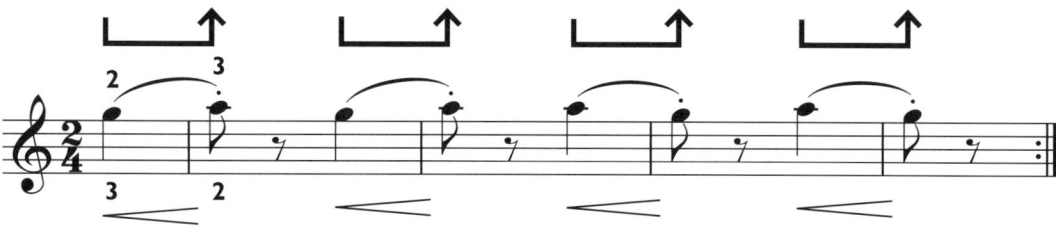

Play this very slowly at first, then a little faster.

Children at play

Now you can use **Spring-offs** to play this great piece by Bartók. The wrist movements will help the piece sound playful.

Practise the melody first at a steady pace with your right hand, then with your left hand, then a little faster.

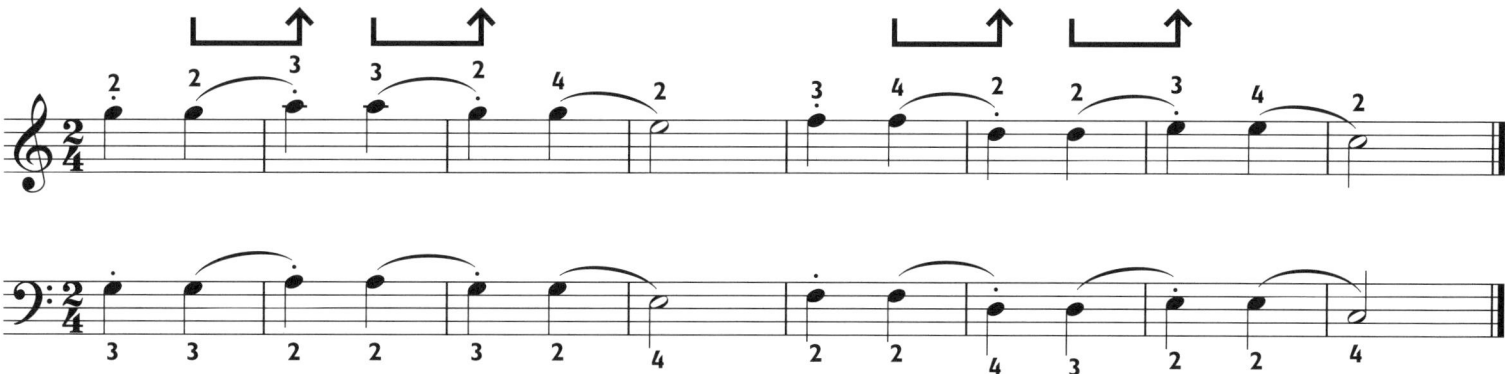

When you feel ready, play 'Children at Play' hands together, with spring-offs in the right hand and rotation in the left hand.

Children at Play

Béla Bartók
arr. Penelope Roskell

Allegro

p semplice

> **Technique Tips**
> ✔ When you play this piece allegro (lively) your wrist won't have time to leap up high. You probably won't even have time to think about an upward movement at all. But your wrist knows what to do by now!

You might also like:

Béla Bartók: 'Children at Play' (No. 1, complete version) and 'My Gift to You' (No. 8) from *For Children* Vol. 1
Charles Gounod: 'Les Pifferari'

Run-ups

Here we'll look at some longer upbeats. It's like doing a run-up before you jump over a fence.

Run and jump

First clap this rhythm with an accent on the JUMP.

run and JUMP   run and JUMP

Keyboard run-ups

Then play a run-up on the piano. Play the last note of each group energetically – press your finger down as your wrist leaps up. The arrows above the notes show you how to move your wrist.

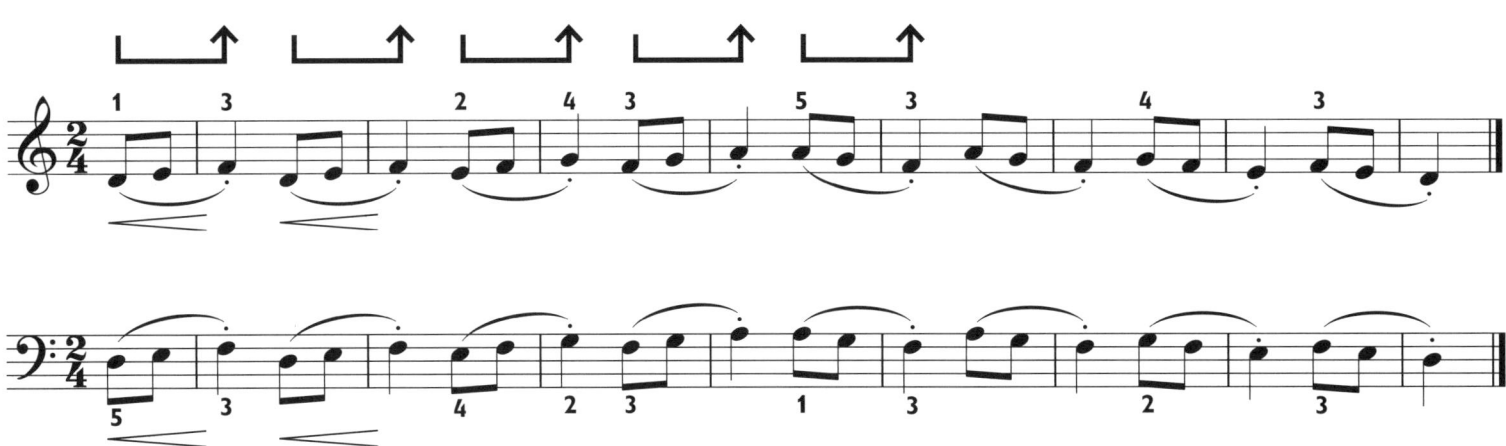

Now play this exercise a little faster. You won't have time to leap up high on every *staccato* note – a small hop is enough. Just listen for the *staccato* and your wrist will know what to do.

Then practise this three-note run-up.

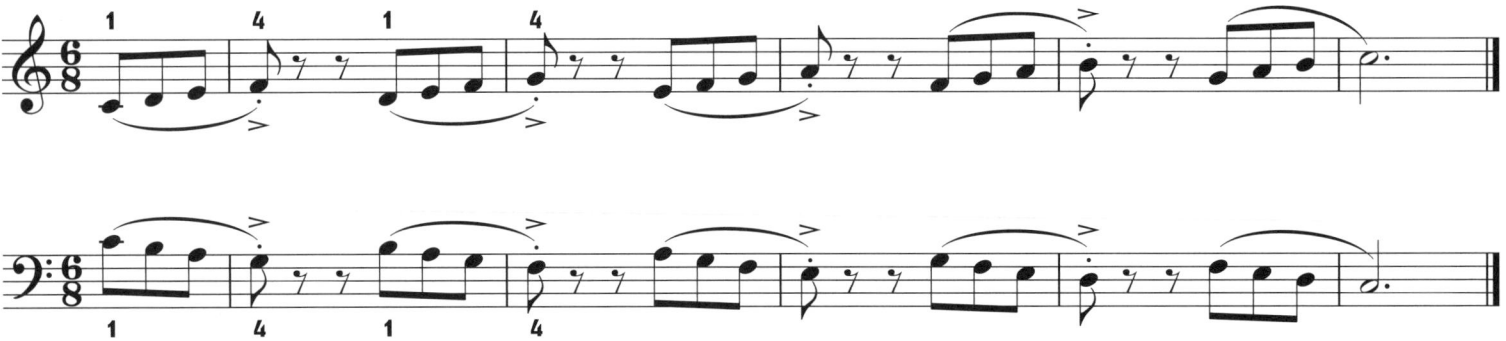

Longer run-ups

Now for a longer run-up! Your wrist can relax down as you play the ♪♪♪♪ then spring up as you play the last note.

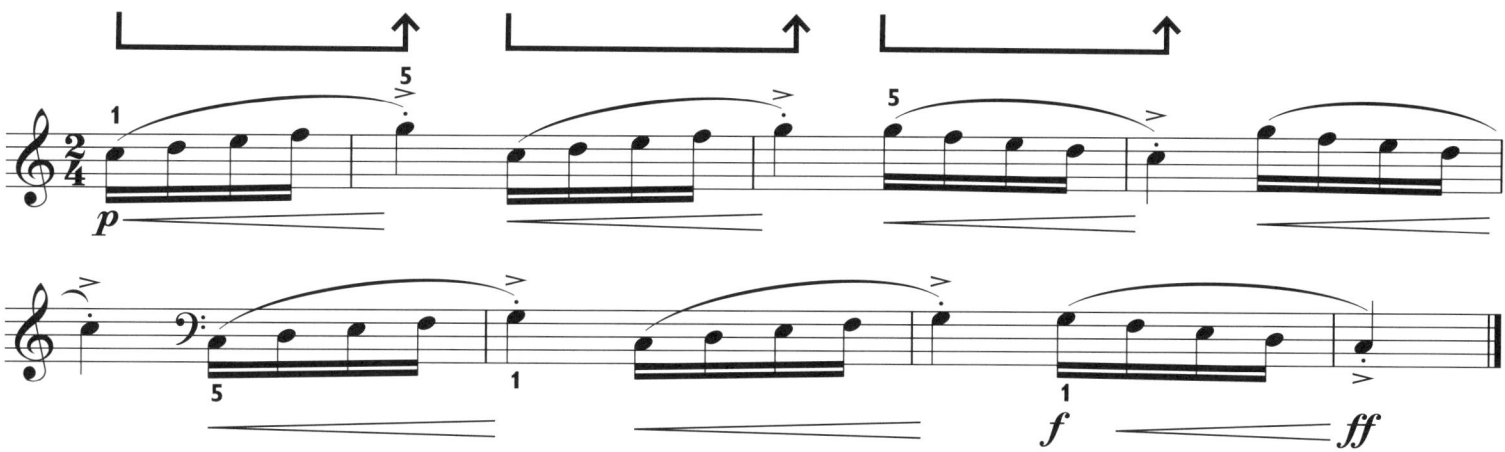

Check out the pattern in this exercise, then play it without looking at the page.

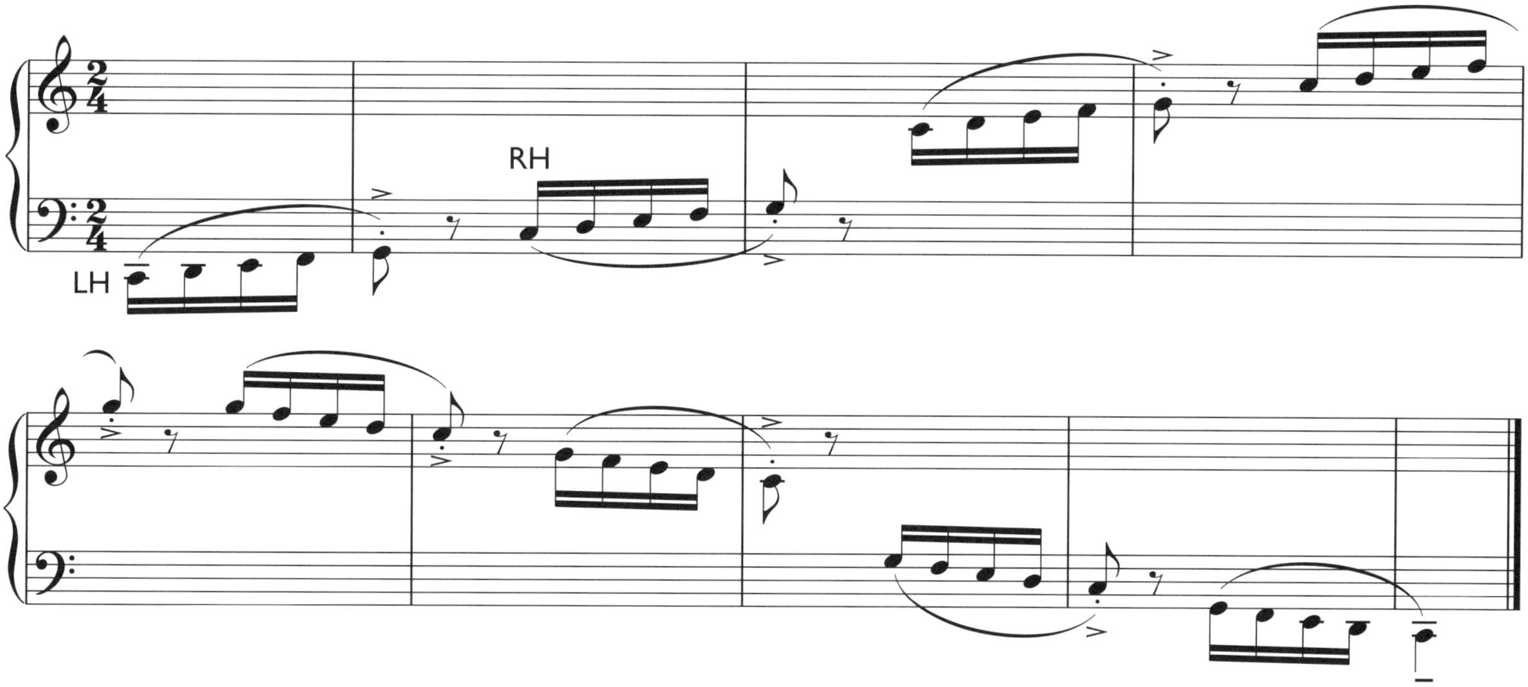

>> Repeat this exercise in other keys, starting with D minor, then A major.

Look out for these techniques in 'Piper's Tune'

Run-ups   Jellyfish jumps   Syncopation with *tenuto*   Longer run-ups

27

Piper's Tune

You may also like:

Johann Hässler: Ecossaise in G Op. 38 No. 23

Dimitri Kabalevsky: 'Clowns' Op. 39 No. 20

Theodor Oesten: 'Spanish Dance' Op. 61 No. 10

Félix Le Couppey: Etude Op. 17 No. 6

Revising techniques

You have already learnt all the techniques for this piece by Joseph Haydn. Look out for:

Tumbling fingers   Upbeats   Syncopated accents   Jellyfish jumps

Thumb on a black note   C minor scale   Jump LAND!

Zingarese

Joseph Haydn
arr. Penelope Roskell

Two-octave arpeggios (left hand)

Arpeggio means 'like a harp'. When a harpist's hands move across the strings, the notes sound like they are shimmering. Similarly, for two-octave arpeggios on the piano, the hands need to flow smoothly across the keyboard, making a rippling sound.

Thumb warm-ups

Place your left hand's third finger on a flat surface. Stretch your thumb out to the side, then slide it smoothly under the third finger and back again. Keep sliding your thumb from side to side – how far can your thumb move comfortably? Keep your arm relaxed as you do this.

Skipping rope

Now at the piano, rest your left hand's third finger on F♯ – think of this finger as a bridge. Swing your thumb under the bridge, feeling your arm swing loosely like a skipping rope to help your thumb reach the notes.

Group 1: Major keys with sharps

Can your thumb reach all the way to the low D in the second bar? Let your skipping-rope arm help you!

Now add in all the notes of the D major arpeggio:

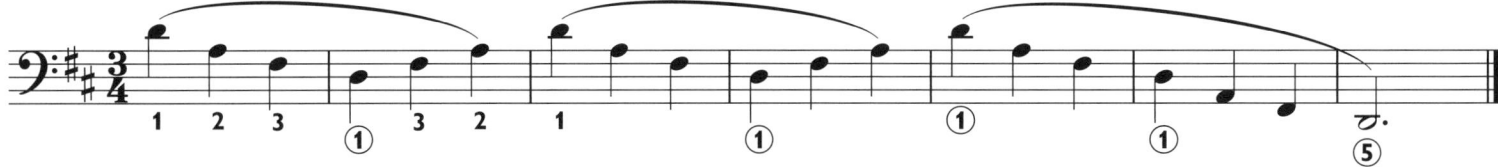

Now play the whole arpeggio, ascending then descending.

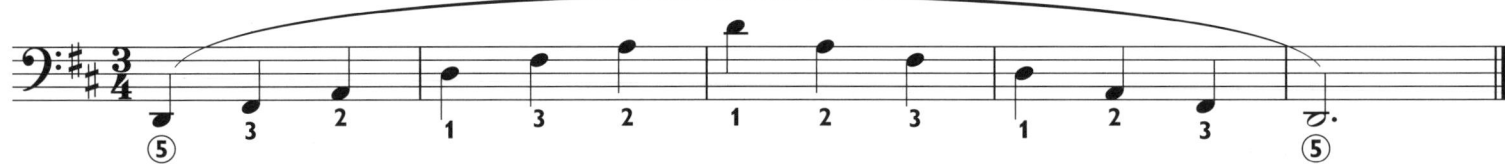

Practise the A and E major arpeggios. You will find them very easy to learn as they feel exactly the same!

Related piece:
Walter Carroll: 'Nightfall' from *Forest Fantasies*

Technique Tip
✔ *Increase the speed of your arpeggios gradually using the Add-a-note technique.*

Left-hand arpeggio groups

The arpeggios in the last chapter (D, A and E major) all have the same combination of white and black notes and share the same fingering. Here we'll look at the two other main groups of arpeggios.

Group 2: Minor keys with flats

The arpeggios in G minor, C minor and F minor can be grouped together as they all feel and look similar. The fourth finger naturally falls on the black note for these arpeggios:

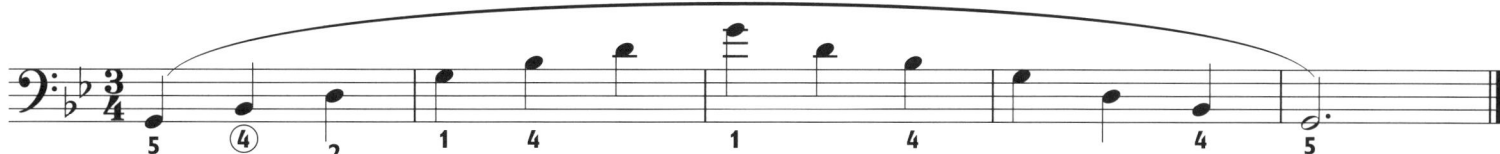

Group 3: White-note arpeggios

D minor only contains white notes:

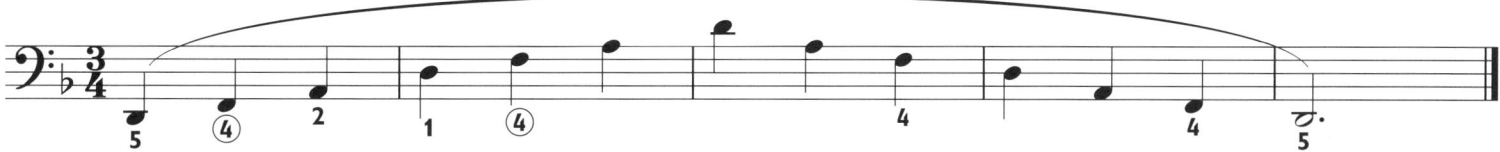

You will now find all the other white key arpeggios – C, G and F major and A and E minor – very easy to play.

The odd ones out!

The arpeggios in B♭ major and B major feel a little different and may need some extra practice:

B♭ major

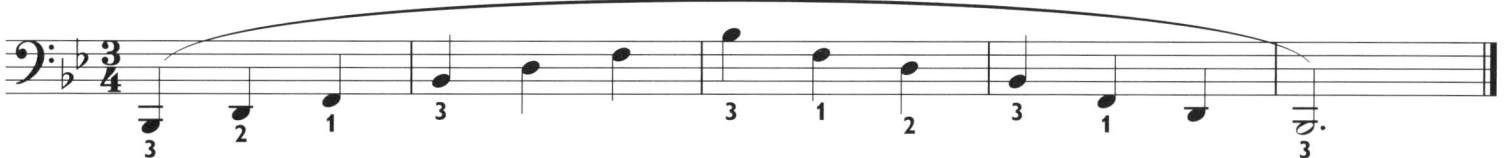

B major

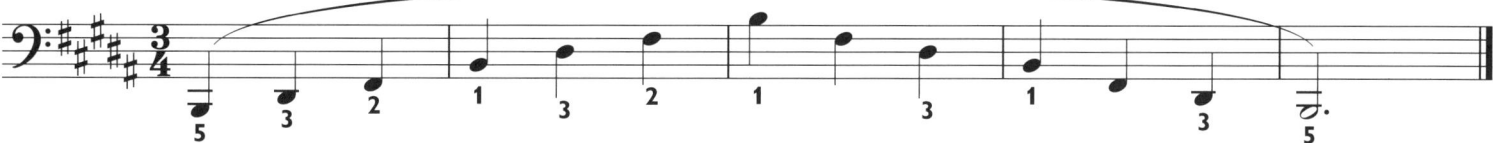

Key	D, A, E major	G, C, F minor	C, G, F major	A, E minor	B♭ major	B major
How many black notes?						
Left hand						

Two-octave arpeggios (right hand)

Here we'll look at arpeggio shapes for the right hand.

Thumb warm-up
Place your right hand's fourth finger on a table and slide your thumb under your hand and back again. Keep your arm relaxed so it helps the thumb slide under.

Skipping-rope technique

Then on your keyboard, hold down F♯ with your fourth finger while your thumb swings loosely under the 'bridge' (your fourth finger). Feel your arm hanging loosely like a rope.

Group 1: Major keys with sharps

In Level 2, you studied one-octave arpeggios. It makes sense to play those starting with the thumb. However, when you play two octaves or more, it's easier and more comfortable to start the arpeggio on your second finger! Your fourth finger plays a black note, and your thumb swings easily underneath using the skipping-rope technique.

Have a go at A major and E major arpeggios with this fingering.

Group 2: Minor keys with flats

Now practise C minor, G minor and F minor. You can use either the third or fourth finger on the black note. Which works better for you?

Group 3: White-note keys

Practise some arpeggios on white keys:

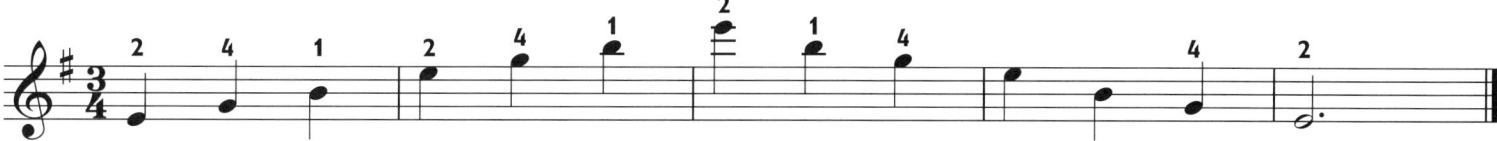

Also practise C, G and F major and A and D minor.

The odd ones out!

B♭ major

B major

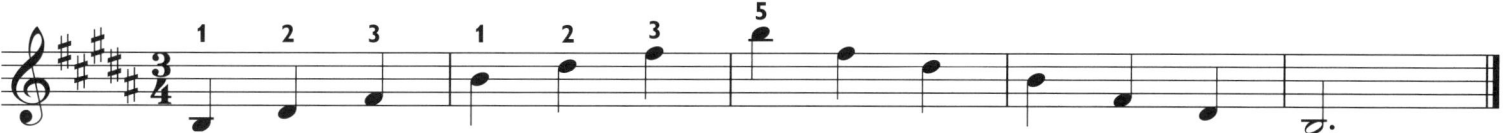

- Each time you learn a new piece, check the key signature. Practise the two-octave scale and arpeggio in that key before learning the piece.
- It's easier to play arpeggios without looking at the music. Look at the notes on the keyboard and plan the fingering before you start.

 **Technique Tips**

✔ Move your whole arm sideways smoothly like a wave.
✘ Don't flap your elbows like chicken wings.
✘ Don't dip your wrist as you play the thumb – just tap your thumb lightly on its corner.

Key	D, A, E major	G, C, F minor	C, G, F major	A, D minor	B♭ major	B major
How many black notes?						
Right hand						
Hands together						

33

Harpist's Serenade

Aaron Burrows

You may also like:

Ludwig van Beethoven: 'Für Elise' (lots of variations on flowing arpeggios!)

Ludwig van Beethoven: Allemande WoO 81 (bars 1–8)

Ignatius Sancho: 'Trip to Dillington' from *12 Country Dances for the Year 1749*

Dynamics explorer

Here are some extreme dynamics for you to try out.

What is the loudest note you can play? Play some loud notes angrily, then joyfully.

What is the quietest note you can play? Play some notes secretively.

Try pressing a key so gently that it doesn't even sound.

Repeat a note with changing dynamics.

Now repeat that note *diminuendo*.

Count how long it takes for a loud note to die away.

Now count how long it takes for a quiet note to die away.

 Make up your own surprising piece using all these extreme dynamics! Don't forget to include some silence.

Cosmic Bells

- Look carefully at the dynamics in this piece.
- Lift your wrist very smoothly after the final chord.

Aaron Burrows

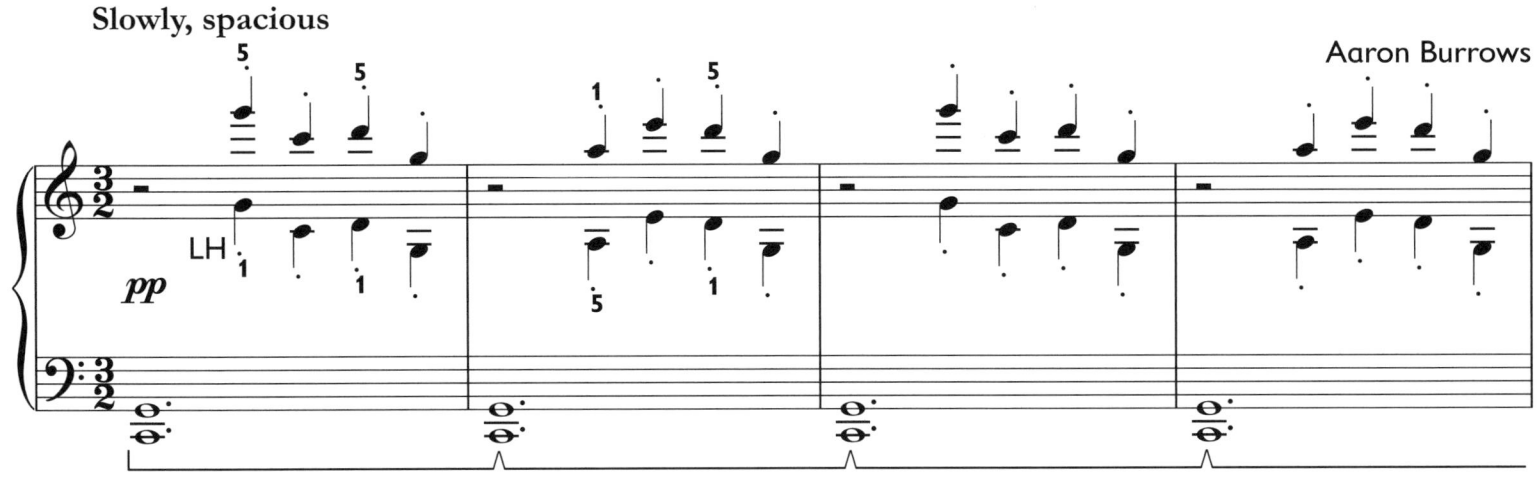

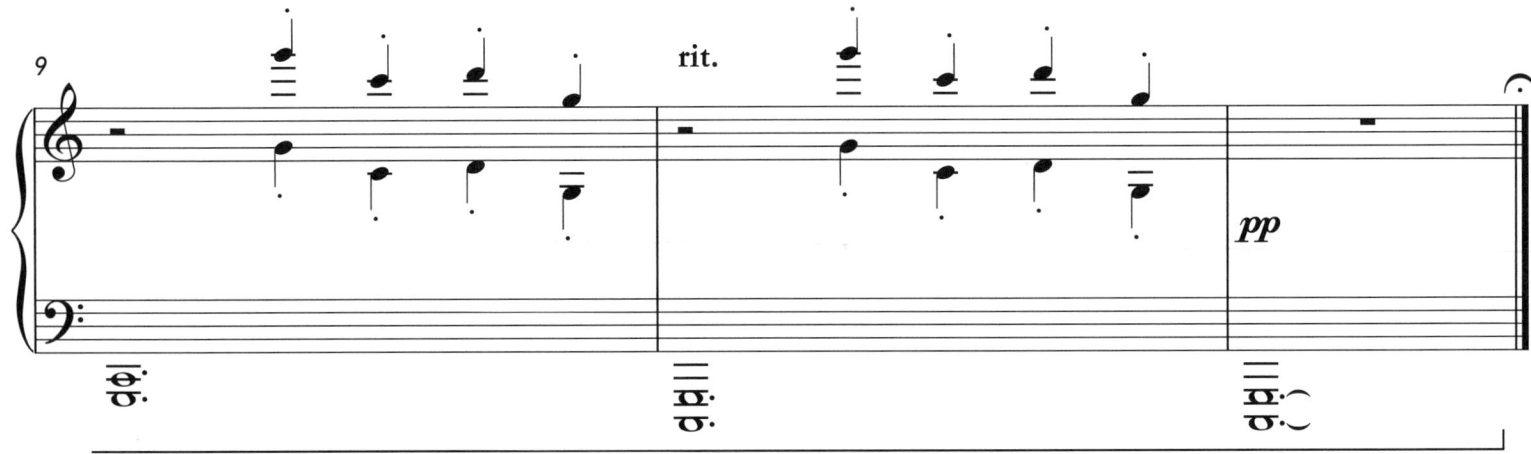

Pianissimo cantabile

Even when playing very quietly (*pianissimo*), great pianists can still be heard clearly in a huge hall. That's because they are playing *pianissimo cantabile*.

Silent stalking

Walk slowly and silently around the room, as if you are stalking a wild animal. Place your feet firmly but gently on the floor so no-one can hear your step! We place our fingers firmly but gently on the keys to play *piano* and *pianissimo*.

Firm but gentle

Sitting down, rest your hand on your leg in its normal rounded playing position. Press your second finger gently but firmly into your leg several times. Then press your third finger, and so on. Close your eyes and notice how it feels as you press each fingertip down into your leg. Then alternate pressing your second and third finger into your leg, as if you are playing *legato*.

Cantabile piano

Repeat the **Firm but gentle** exercises at the piano, playing *piano*:

Walking *pianissimo*

At the piano, parachute down slowly and gently to land on D with your second finger, feeling your finger sink down to the bottom of the key.

Then walk from finger 2 to finger 3, *pianissimo*. Keep feeling both fingers press down to the bottom of the key. Practise this *piano*, then *pianissimo*. Lift your hand very gradually on the last note, as you did in **Elegant endings** (p. 9).

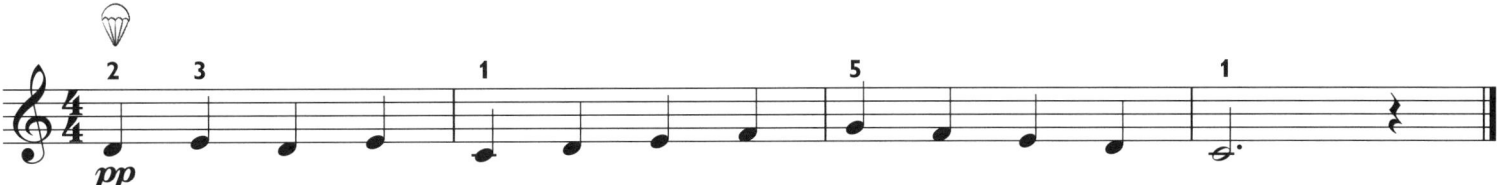

Walk *pianissimo* with your left hand.

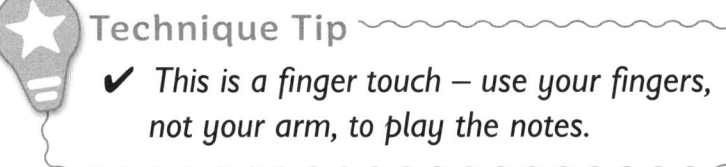

Technique Tip

✔ *This is a finger touch — use your fingers, not your arm, to play the notes.*

Valse

Use *pianissimo cantabile* touch to play 'Valse'.

Aaron Burrows

[Sheet music: Lent, 3/4, pp, with retenu and ppp markings]

- Remember to lift your hand very smoothly from the final chord.

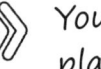 You might like to revisit these pieces and practise playing each one pianissimo cantabile:

A Journey through the Snow (Primer A, p.38);
Orbit and **Whimsy** (Level 2 p. 14, p. 22)

Melody and accompaniment

A piano piece usually sounds more beautiful when the melody sings out a little more loudly than the accompaniment. These exercises will help you work on this balance between your hands.

Elephant and bird

Drop your right hand heavily onto your leg and mime a pentascale. Feel your fingers pressing heavily into your leg, like an elephant.

Now rest your left hand lightly on your head and mime playing a very quiet pentascale. Mime **Echo**, below, on your leg and head. Can you feel your right hand pressing more deeply into your leg?

Echo

This exercise will help you work on this balance between your hands.

Repeat each two-bar phrase until it feels easy. If you find it hard to play *pianissimo* at first, aim for *piano*.

Melody

In 'Melody' by Robert Schumann, the right hand needs to sing while the left hand plays the accompaniment a little more quietly.

- Play the right hand *mf* cantabile while your teacher plays the left hand *pp*.
- Play the left hand *pp* while your teacher plays the right hand *mf* cantabile.
- 🎵 Listen carefully – does the balance of the sounds seem just right?

Now imagine that your right hand is a singer, and your left is a shy accompanist who likes to stay in the background. Play this piece hands together as expressively as you can!

Robert Schumann

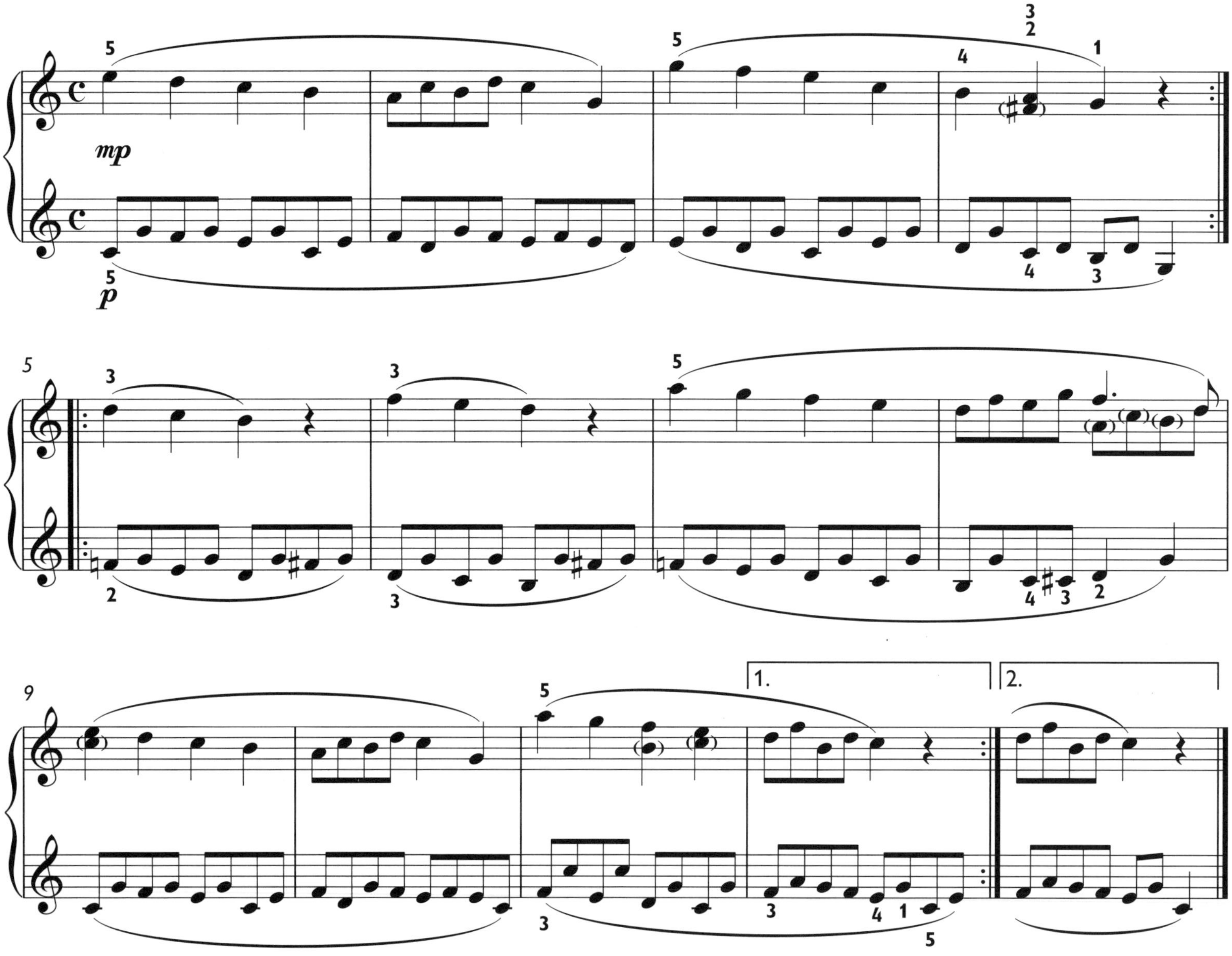

>> Can you make the right hand sing more than the left hand in these pieces from the previous books?

Level 1, p. 55: **Little Piece** by Robert Schumann

Level 2, p. 39: **Sonatine** by Thomas Attwood

Left-hand melodies

Piano pieces with the main melody in the left hand tend to sound rich and expressive.

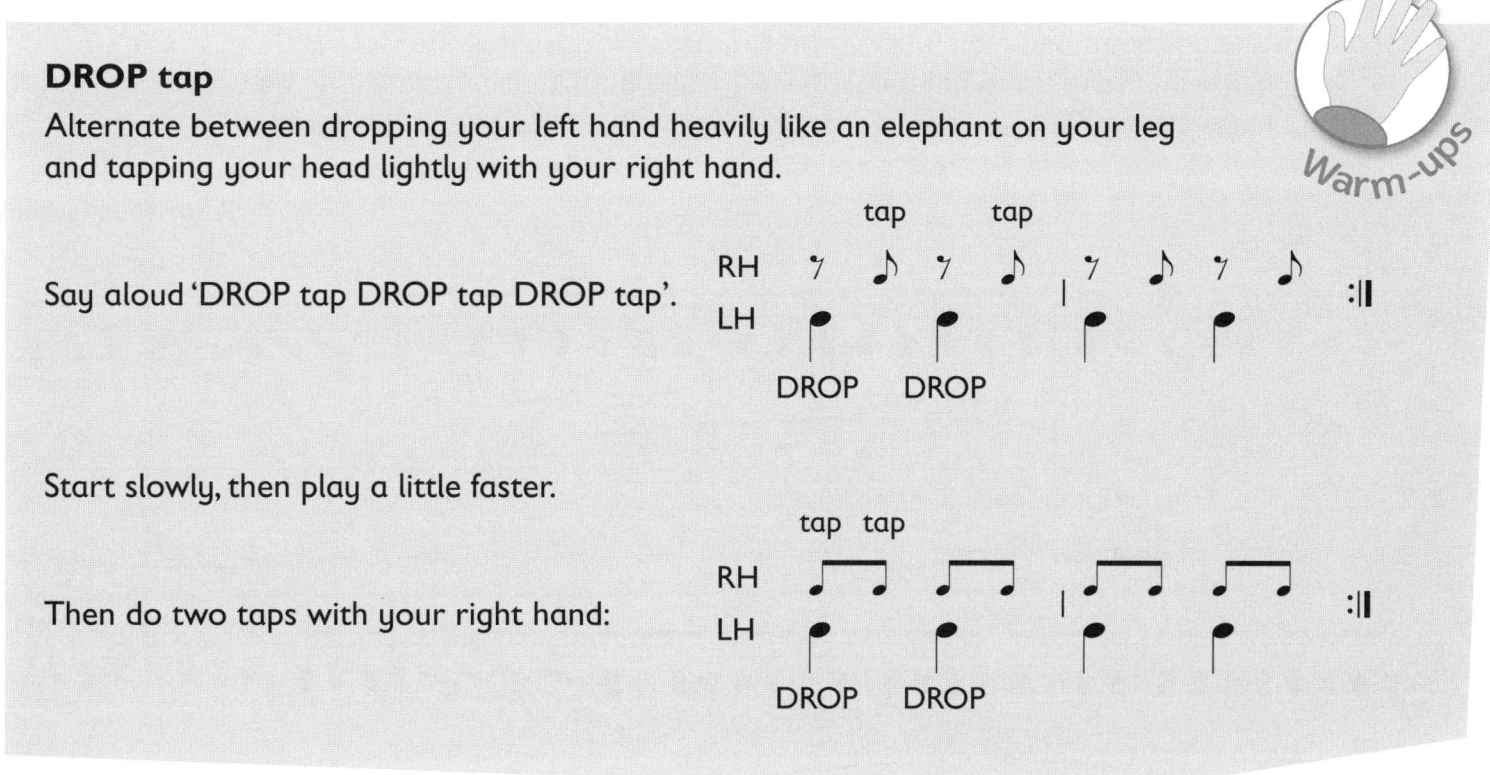

Ghost

Now play this ghostly exercise at the piano, playing the right hand very lightly throughout:

Night Journey

 Listening is a vital part of piano technique. Listen to your teacher playing 'Night Journey'. Can you hear the left hand playing the melody all the way through the piece?

- Learn the left hand and play it firmly while your teacher plays the top part.
- Then learn the right hand and play it gently while your teacher plays the melody, *cantabile*.
- Then learn the whole piece hands together. Keep listening to your left hand!

Cornelius Gurlitt

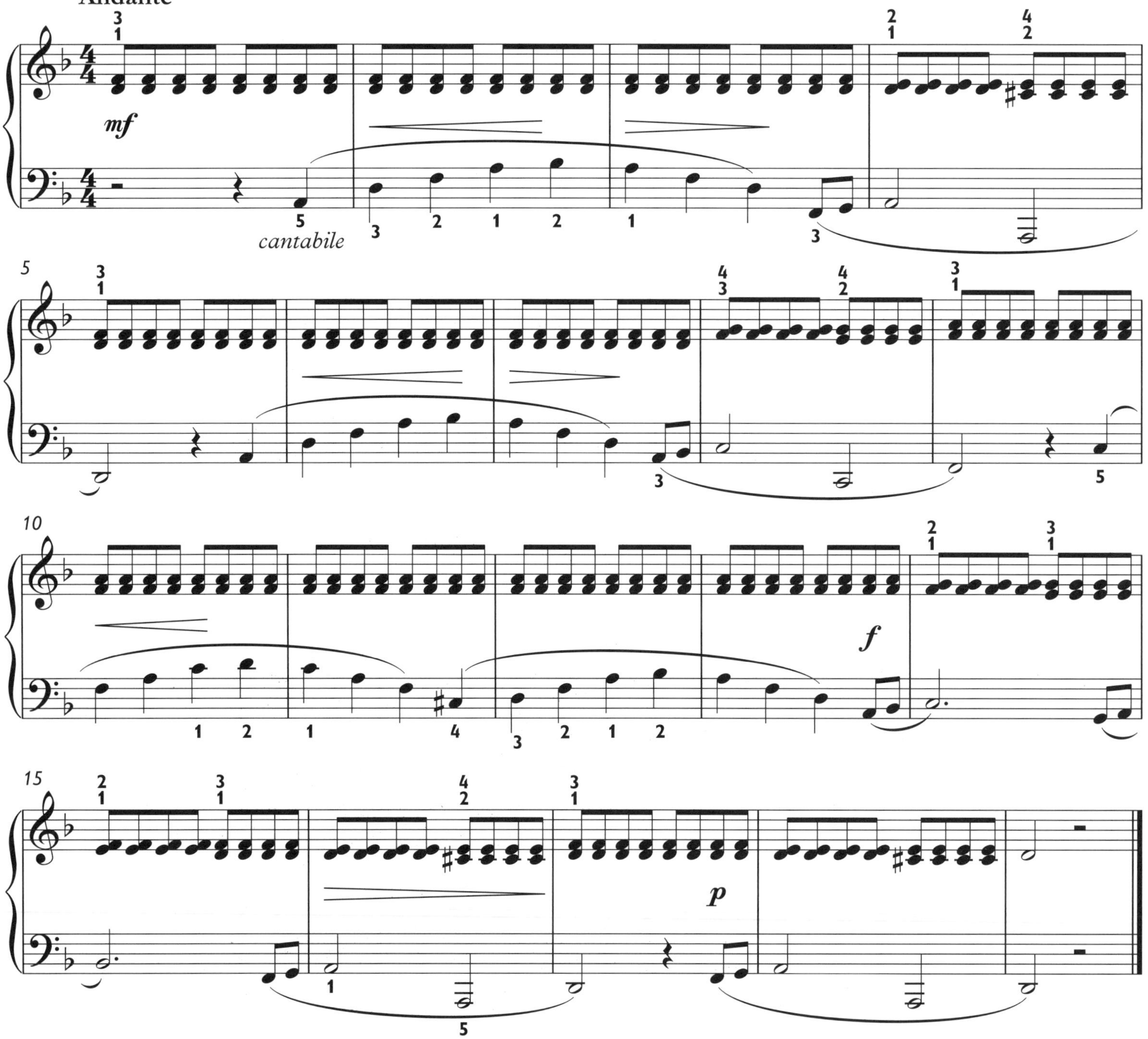

You may like to revisit:
Level 2: 'In the Garden' (p. 32)
Level 3: 'Elegy' (p. 23)

You may also like:
Robert Schumann: 'The Happy Farmer' from *Album for the Young*
Hywel Davis (arr.): 'O Waly Waly'

Wide leaps

The exercises in this section will help you move freely around the keyboard to find the notes confidently and accurately.

 **Pot of gold**
Draw some large rainbow shapes in the air in front of you with your left hand, then with your right hand, and pretend you are dropping a pot of gold at each end of the rainbow.

Then draw the shape of some hills in the distance, slowly then more quickly.

Leaping octaves

Play all the Cs across the keyboard with the third finger of the right hand, then the left hand. Then practise the exercise below, first with just the third finger, then with the fingering shown. Practise these leaps until your arm develops a muscle memory of how far it needs to move to take the fingers to the right notes.

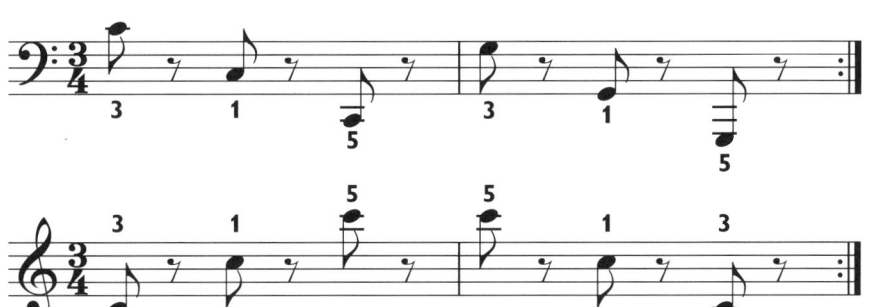

 **Technique Tips**
✔ Don't stretch out between your thumb and fifth finger. Keep your hand compact so your arm is firmly behind each finger as it plays.

Playing from memory

It is much easier to play leaps accurately if you know the notes from memory. Before learning 'Prelude', practise this exercise to help you memorise the right-hand chords so you will be able to focus on the leaps in the left hand.

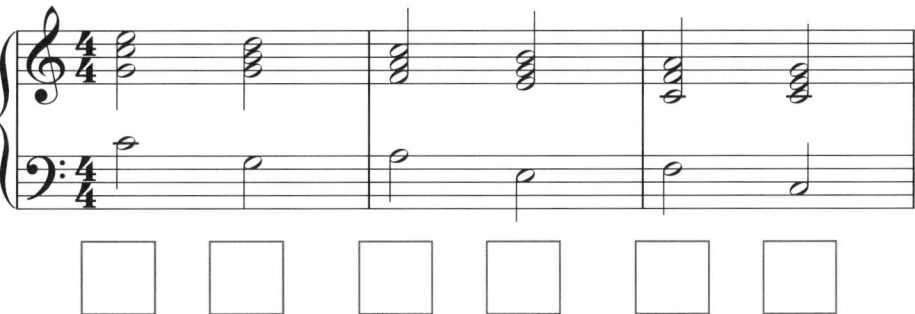

The left-hand notes are the roots of the chords. Write in the chord names and say these aloud while you practise playing them from memory. The chords may sound familiar as they are the same as in 'Pachelbel's Canon' from Level 1.

Prelude

- Look carefully at the dynamics. Play *forte* with grand arm arches – drop heavily onto each note. Play *piano* with a much gentler bobbing technique.

Moderately

E. Tetsel

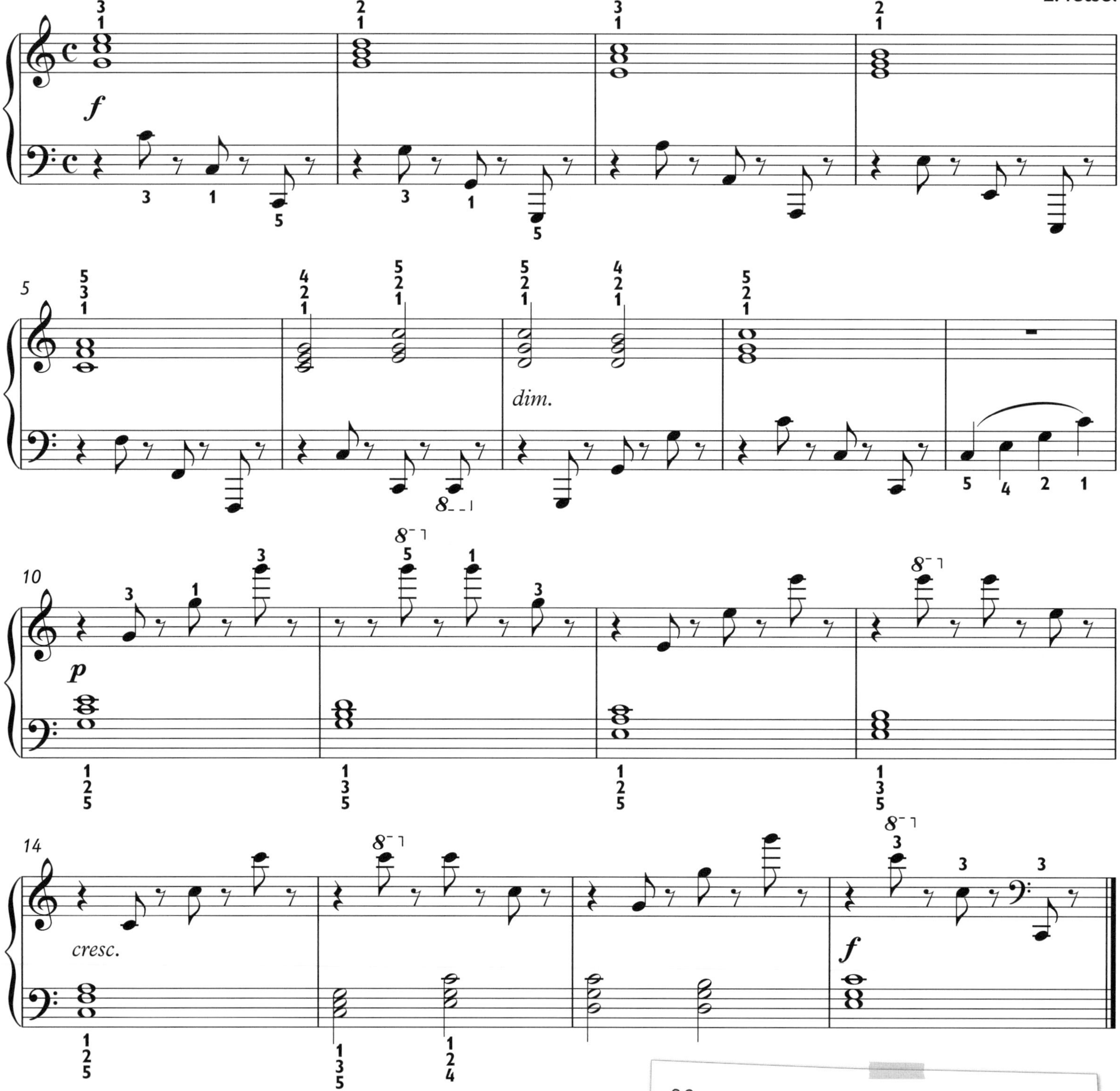

You might also like:

Béla Bartók: 'Round Dance' from *For Children* Vol. 1, No. 17
Frédéric Chopin: Prelude Op. 28 No. 7

>> This piece also sounds good with legato pedalling. Change the pedal at the beginning of every bar.

Duplets and triplets

In this chapter we'll explore good technique for playing duplets and triplets.

Pears, oranges and pineapples

With your teacher, clap a steady ♩ as you say aloud:

| ta | ta | ti - ri | ti - ri | ta | ta | tri - o - la | ta |
| Pear | pear | o - range | o - range | pear | pear | pine - ap - ple | pear |

Can you find your own words for these rhythms? Perhaps the names of animals, or places nearby? Make up your own exercise including duplets and triplets.

Duplets and triplets

As you play this exercise, drop your wrist to play the main beats more heavily and lift it slightly to lighten the other notes.

Now play this without dropping your wrist on the beat.

Triplets in Lydian Mode

Play this duet by Béla Bartók with your teacher. You may find it helps to say aloud *tiri* and *triola* (or *orange* and *pineapple*) at first to help with the rhythms.

Swap parts with your teacher. Feel the movement of your left hand keeping the steady beat.

Call and response

Make up your own **Call and response** using the same five notes, including these rhythms:

Repeated notes

If you repeat a note over and over with the same finger it can sound very boring.
Repeated notes sound more interesting if you change finger on each note.
Use your arm to support the finger change.

Sideways bounce

Start by dropping your fourth finger onto a note like a bouncing ball. Then move your hand sideways and play the same note with your thumb. Bounce your arm from side to side as you change fingers.

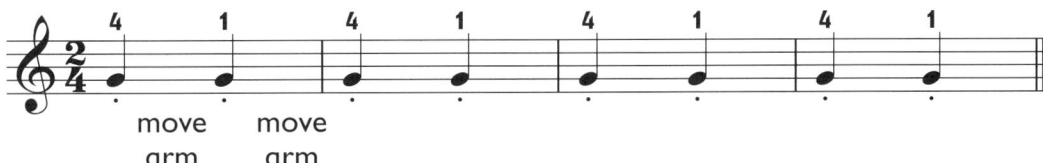

Now add the fingers in between. Let your hand shift sideways as you change from finger to finger.

Jumping on the steps

SECONDO (Teacher part)

Play It Again

Aaron Burrows

You might also like:

Seymour Bernstein: 'The Elegant Toreador'

Dmitry Kabalevsky: 'Playing Ball' Op. 27 No. 5

Lajos Papp: 'Zither' and 'Trumpet Waltz' from *22 Little Piano Pieces*

Blanche K. Thomas (arr.): 'Steal Away' and 'Swing Low, Sweet Chariot' from *Plantation Songs in Easy Arrangements*

PRIMO (Student part)

Play It Again

Play one octave higher than written throughout.

Aaron Burrows

Joyfully!

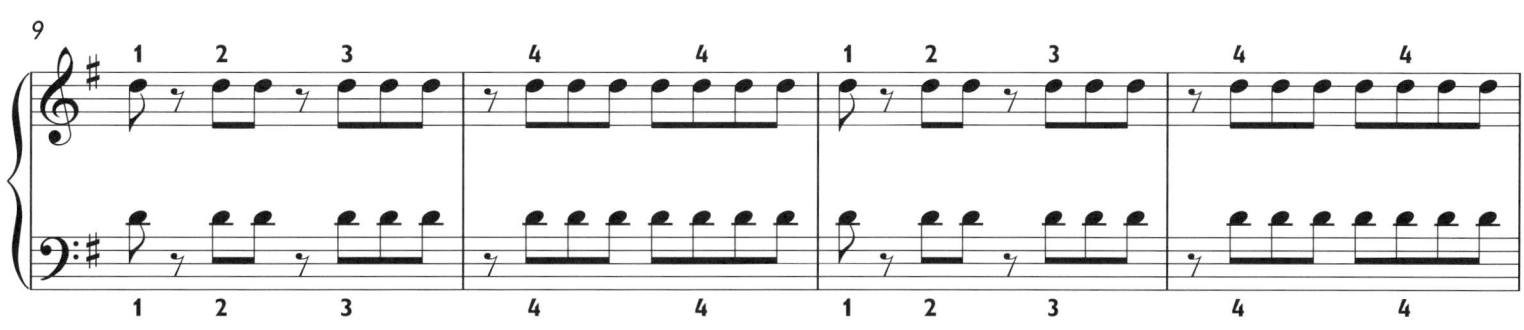

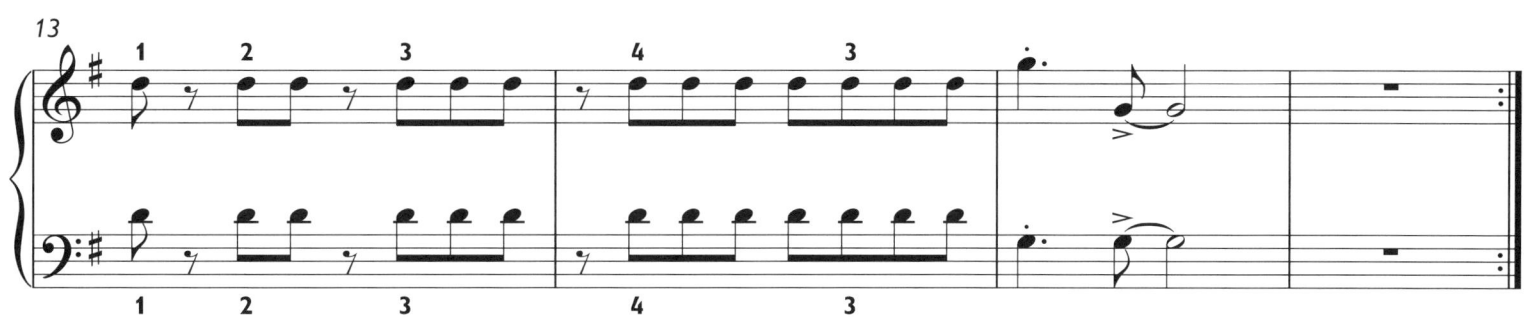

Repeated chords

Here you'll learn a simple bouncing movement to help you repeat chords easily.

Bouncy ball

Compare dropping your hand onto your leg first like a floppy beanbag, then like a bouncy ball.

Keep bouncing your hand on your leg in a steady rhythm like a bouncy ball. Bounce slowly at first, then more quickly.

Light bouncing

Now at the piano bounce lightly onto each fifth, then keep repeating the fifth with a light bounce.

Throwing your hand

Pretend you are throwing a ball in front of you. Then throw your hand onto your leg.

Throw your hand onto a fifth on the keyboard as in the first bar (measure) of the exercise below. This throwing action will give the required accent.

Now throw your hand again and let the fifth repeat. Imagine that your hand is a ball that just keeps on bouncing by itself after being thrown.

The New Doll

The left hand bounces lightly on the repeated chords in this piece by Tchaikovsky.

- Feel your left hand and arm relax during the rests.

Pyotr Ilyich Tchaikovsky

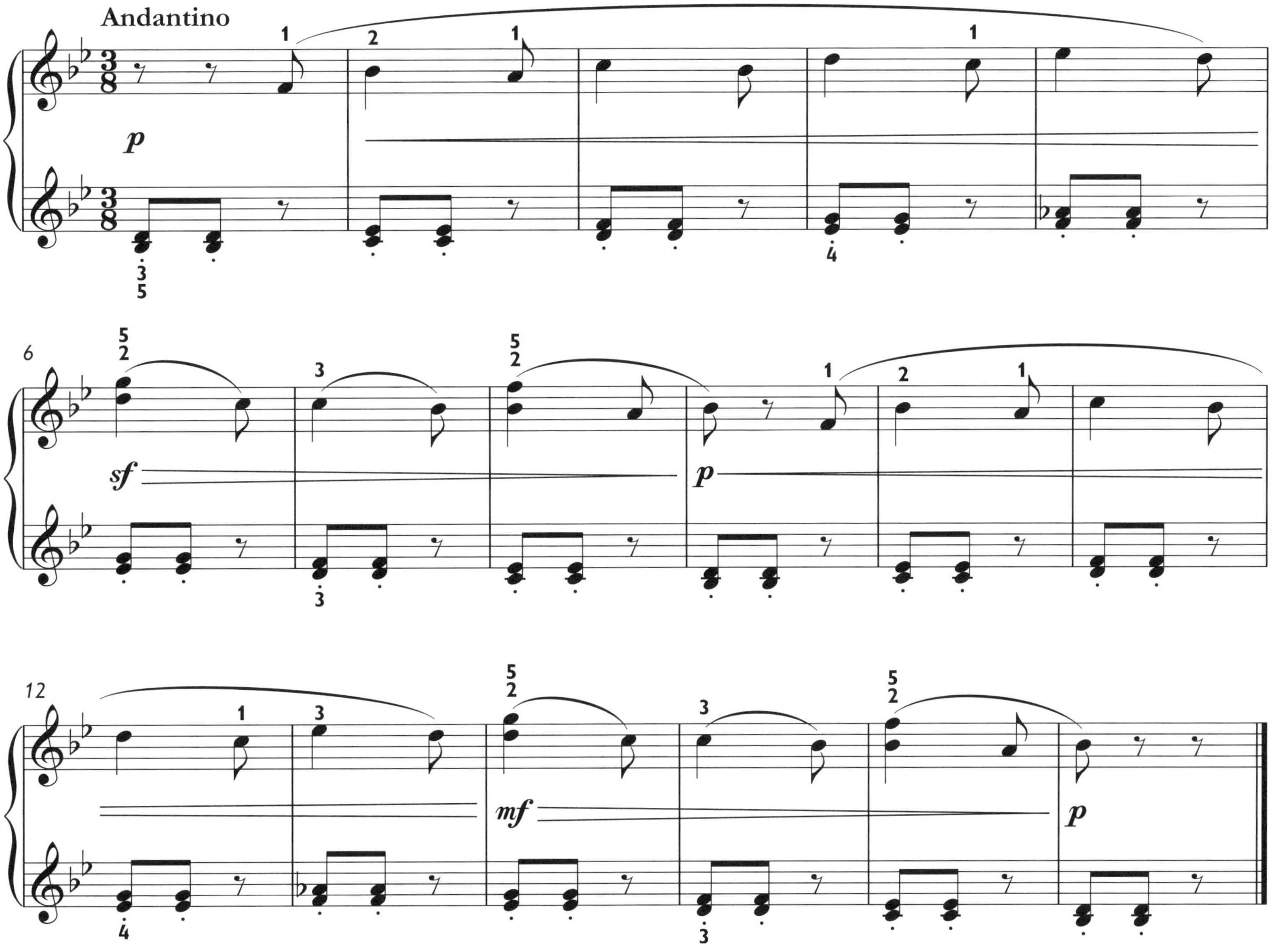

You might also like:

Alexander Goedicke: No. 15 from *20 Little Pieces for Beginners* Op. 6
Béla Bartók: 'Study for the Left Hand' from *For Children*, Vol. 1 No. 6
Samuel Maykapar: 'In the Garden'
Wynn-Anne Rossi: 'El reggae jamaicano' (duet)

Celebration Dance

In this piece throw your hands onto all the accented chords.

Aaron Burrows

Combining techniques

Look out for these techniques:

Repeated single notes   Repeated thirds   Accents   One-octave arpeggios

Fanfare Minuet

Fanfares are usually played by trumpets and sound very joyful. Play this piece boldly.

William Duncombe

Mordents

The word mordent means *biting* — a mordent adds a bit of spice to a note. Simple three-note mordents include the written note, plus the note *above*.

A mordent can be written like this:

   or like this:

Cloud hands

Mordents should be played with a light touch. Move your hands lightly in the air in front of you like clouds, twiddling your fingers as you do this.

Twiddly fingers

Then place your hands very lightly on a table. Twiddle all your fingers lightly on the surface, as if you were tapping on a laptop. Then alternate only the second and third finger.

Now tap your thumb neatly on the surface — how quickly can you do this? Alternate your thumb and third finger, tapping lightly.

Three-note mordents

Practise a mordent steadily at first, starting on the beat. Play with your thumb and third finger.

Now repeat this exercise, playing the mordent with your second and third finger.

Speedy flutters

Now sneak the mordent in quickly *before* the beat:

Grandmother's Minuet

- Sneak the mordent in before the beat.
- Keep your arm light and twiddle your fingers.

Edvard Grieg
arr. Penelope Roskell

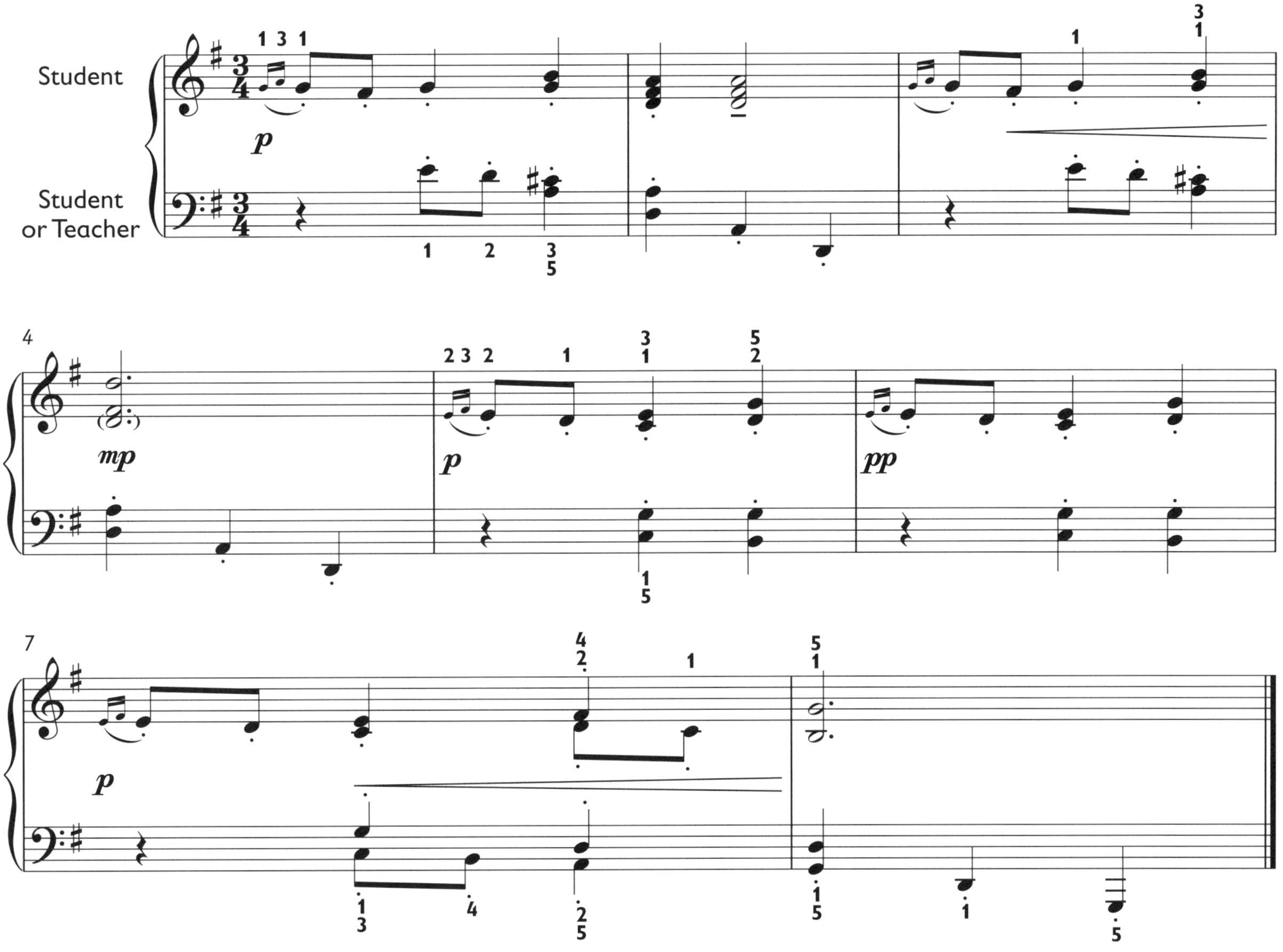

You might also like:

William Gillock: 'The Spanish Guitar'

Jakub Metelka: 'Little Dancer' from *Modern Piano Studies*

Trills

When you add more notes to a mordent, it becomes a trill.

𝆡 = mordent = ♫

tr = ♬♬ or ♬♬♬♬

You don't need to press heavily into the piano keyboard when you play trills.

Laptop warm-up

Try tapping on a laptop as lightly as you can. Don't waste energy by pressing heavily. Twiddle your fingers lightly in the air, then on a flat surface.

Short trills

First practise playing short trills with these different fingerings:

Now try adding a few more notes for a longer trill:

The Trickster

Allegro moderato

Aaron Burrows

You might also like:

Jason Noble: 'Wasps' from *RCM Celebration Series*
Vitalij Neugasimov: 'Lazy Bear' from *Piano Sketches Book 1*
Agnieszka Lasko: 'A Very Worried Bee'

Technique Tips

✔ *Don't press into the keys! Float down onto the keyboard, twiddle your fingers lightly, then float off at the end.*
✔ *Keep your arm light and tickle the keys delicately with your fingers.*

Inverted mordents

 Inverted mordents are upside-down mordents. They also have three notes – but here the middle note is the note below.

Droplets

Start by practising an inverted mordent on the beat:

Technique Tips
- Parachute very lightly onto the first note and float off at the end.
- Feel your hand become as soft as a jellyfish in between the ornaments.

Then sneak it in very quickly before the beat:

Also practise these mordents with second and third fingers.

Menuet in D Minor

This piece by Elizabeth Jacquet de la Guerre includes both mordents and inverted mordents.

Elisabeth Jacquet de la Guerre
arr. Penelope Roskell

You might also like:

Elisabeth Jacquet de la Guerre: Menuet in D Minor (complete version)

J.S. Bach: 'Polonaise' from *Anna Magdalene Notebook* BWV Anh 128 No. 24

Relaxed hand and fingers

Have you ever noticed your fingers sticking up in the air when they're not playing a note? That's a waste of energy! Your fingers need some down time. When they aren't actually playing, they should rest on the surface of the keys.

Down time

Parachute down to land with your second finger on your leg. Do all the other fingers feel soft and relaxed? Parachute onto your third finger. Again, check the other fingers stay relaxed and don't stick up. Can you do the same with your fourth and fifth fingers?

Time for a rest

Now at the piano, practise this exercise for relaxing sticking up fifth fingers:

Feel the flop

As you rest on each long note, relax your hand and let the other fingers flop and rest lightly on the key surface:

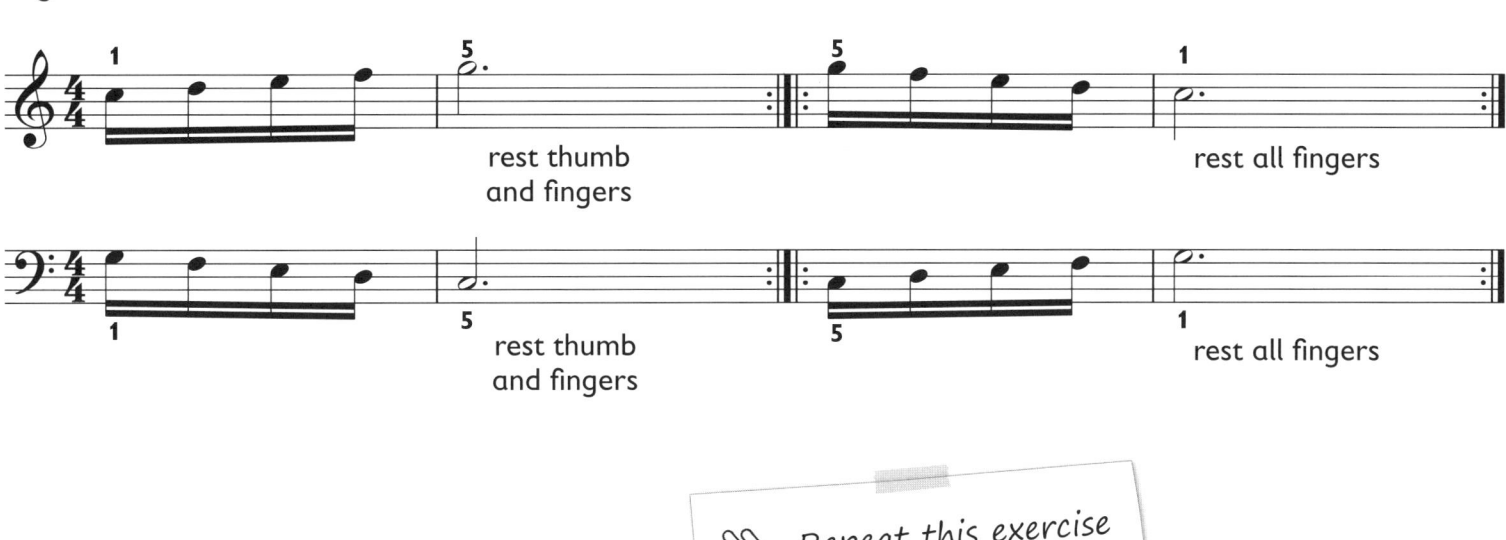

>> Repeat this exercise in different keys

Quiet hand

In this exercise, check that your fingers rest lightly on the key surface whenever they are not playing. Play each hand separately several times before playing hands together.

You might also like:
Lajos Papp: 'Ball Game', No. 16 from *22 Little Piano Pieces*
Dmitry Kabalevsky: No. 22 from *24 Pieces for Children* Op. 39

Held notes

Sometimes one finger needs to hold a note down while the other fingers play *staccato*. This can produce very interesting musical textures.

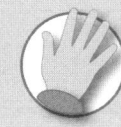

Thumb circles
Rest your fifth finger on a flat surface while you draw large circles in the air with your thumb. Keep your arm light and let it move with your thumb.

Warm-ups

Resting on your fifth finger

Play a D on the piano with the fifth finger of your right hand and move your thumb around in circles. Don't press your fifth finger forcefully into the key – keep your hand light and loose.

Start to tap the thumb:

Technique Tips
✓ *Play on the thumb corner.*

Then add in the other fingers:

Now try this exercise in the left hand:

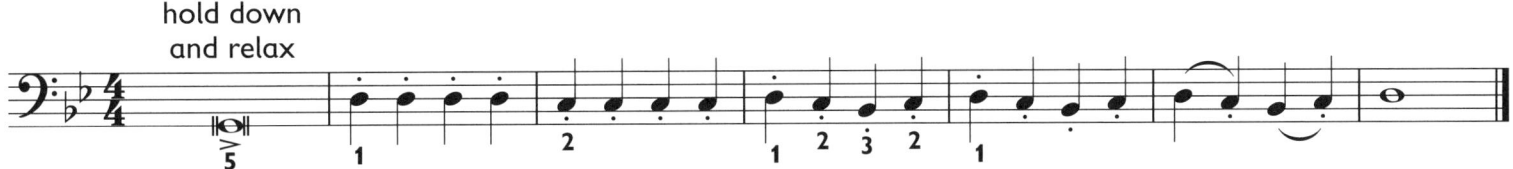

Play this *piano*, then *mezzo piano*, then *mezzo forte*.

I Danced With a Pig

Practise the first eight bars of this piece hands separately, then, when you are ready, hands together. The piece has two names – 'Swineherd's Dance' and 'I Danced With a Pig'!

- It's important not to get tense while you play this! Play with a light, bouncing action on all the *staccato* notes.
- Don't press your fifth finger down into the key.

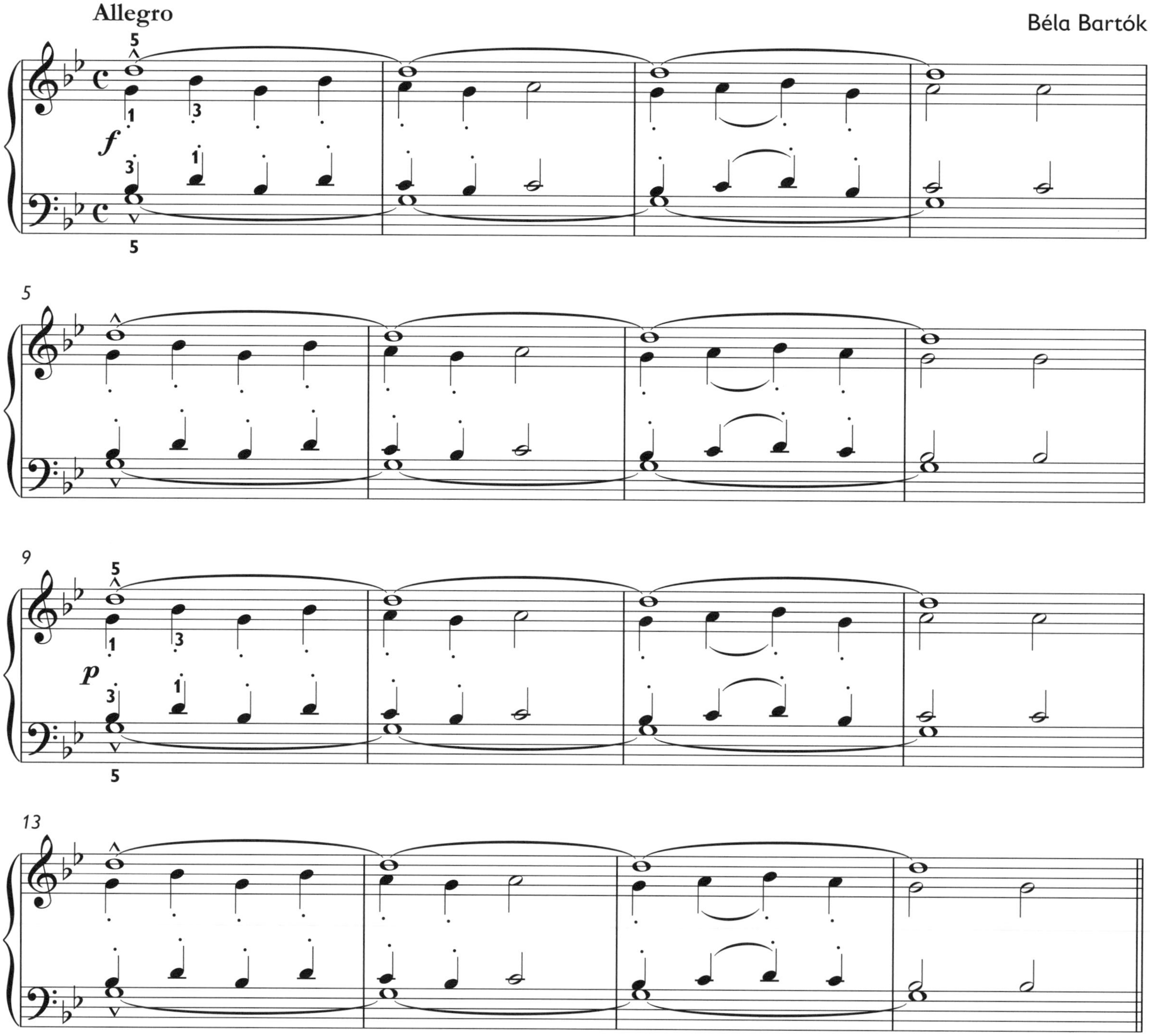

Allegro

Béla Bartók

Resting thumb

 **Hand circles**
Rest your thumb lightly on your leg or on a flat surface and move your hand around in the air in circles. Still resting on your thumb, tap lightly with your fifth finger.

Resting on your thumb

Play the first note with an accent, then give your hand a wiggle to relax your thumb and fingers. Let your thumb rest lightly on the note while your other fingers play *staccato*.

Now you are ready to play the second half of 'I Danced With a Pig':

Béla Bartók

Now play both halves of 'I Danced With a Pig' without stopping.

You might also like:

Pyotr Ilyich Tchaikovsky: 'Old French Song'

Samuel Maykapar: 'Pedal Prelude' No. 11

Robert Schumann: 'Cradle Song' from *Twenty Piano Pieces* Op. 124

June Armstrong: 'Giraffes Loping' from *Safari: Adventures for Piano*

Legato thirds

Here we'll look at how to play thirds (intervals three notes apart) with a smooth, singing tone.

 **Even landings**
Imagine your hand is a parachutist landing on two feet. Parachute onto your knee, landing on your second and fourth finger. Do both fingers land firmly at the same time? Repeat, landing on your thumb and third finger, then on your third and fifth fingers.

Cantabile thirds

Your fingers are like pillars that support your hand. Each time you play a third, check that the weight of your hand is well balanced on both pillars.

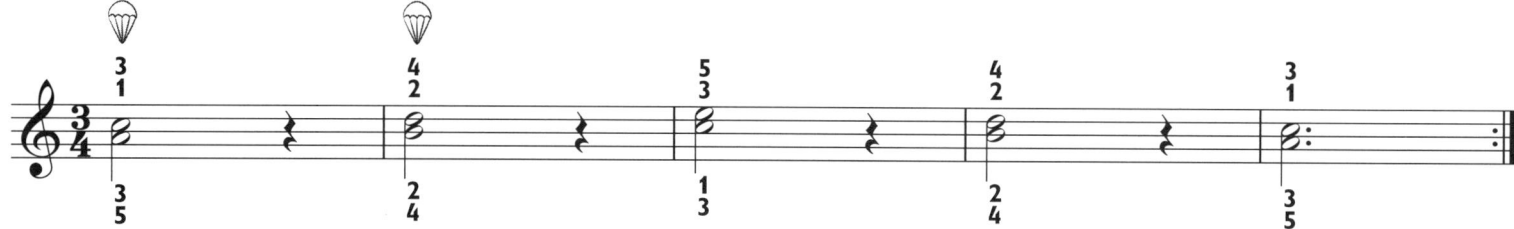

Slurred thirds

Now slur the thirds together, using the wrist movement shown.

 **Technique Tips**
- ✔ When playing legato thirds, only raise your wrist during the rests.
- ✔ Listen to make sure that both notes go down together.
- ✔ Relax non-playing fingers.

Thirds Against a Single Voice

Andante ♩ = 110

Béla Bartók

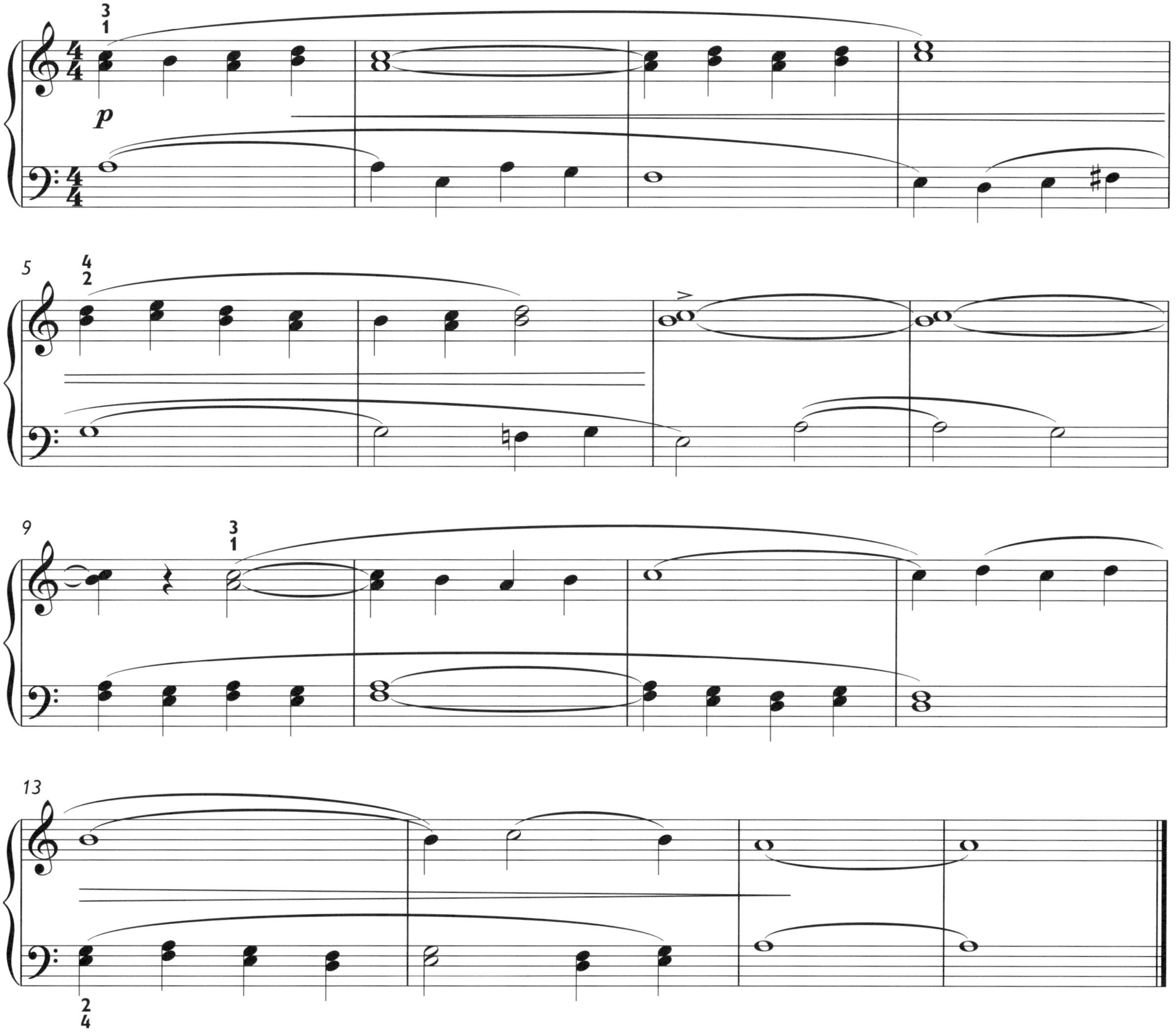

You might also like:

Lajos Papp: 'Waltz 11' from *22 Little Piano Pieces*

Petr Eben (arr.): 'Roses at the Cottage Window'

Direct pedalling

In Level 2, you learnt *legato* pedalling. Here you will learn direct pedalling. Your foot goes down *as you play the note*.

Alligator

Rest your heel on the floor and flap your foot up and down from the ankle like an alligator's mouth.

Then count out loud as you flap your foot up and down in rhythm:

1	2	3		1	2	3
Down		Up		Down		Up

Place your foot over the right (sustaining) pedal and count the same rhythm as your foot moves up and down.

Direct pedalling

Now play the first two bars of this exercise, pressing the pedal down on the first beat of each bar and up on the third. Be careful not to pedal through the rest on the third beat.

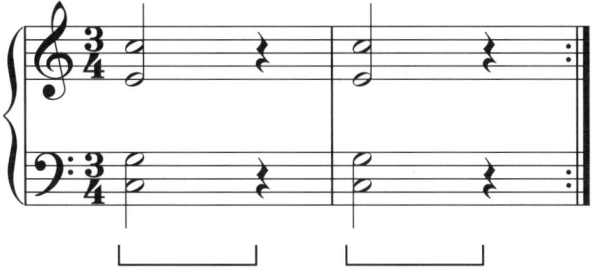

Then play the complete exercise.

etc.

Technique Tips

✗ *Never press so heavily you can hear your foot thud on the pedal.*
✔ *Make a smooth neat movement with your foot – don't snatch at it.*

Sad at Heart

This piece uses the same direct pedalling as the exercises on the previous page.
Be careful not to pedal through the rests – lift your foot on the third beat of each bar.

You might also like:

Samuel Maykapar: No. 2 in E minor, from *20 Pedal Preludes* Op. 38

SECONDO (Teacher part)

Hat Tip Polka

Aaron Burrows

Con brio

Teaching notes

- **R** = Revision
- **LO** = Learning Objectives
- **TT** = Teaching Tips
- **RP** = Related Pieces, either from *Essential Piano Technique*, or other recommended repertoire which is readily available.

 Video demonstrations can be accessed via the QR code, or by visiting www.fabermusic.com/ep/essential-piano-technique

Page 5 — Warm-up routine

- **R** Sitting posture (Level 2, p. 7); The swan landing (*The Complete Pianist*, p. 67).
- **LO** To relax the shoulders and arms and establish a regular and effective warm up routine before practice.
- **TT** These exercises engage the stronger muscles of the upper arm and shoulder which are then used to support the weight of the arm at the keyboard.

Page 6 — Tumbling fingers

- **R** Floating off (Level 1, p. 36); Down-ups (Primer B, p. 18); Wavy broken chords (Primer B, p. 25); Mexican Wave (*The Complete Pianist*, pp. 97–99).
- **LO** To develop a fast, light, finger action within flowing, scooping arm movements.
- **TT** Aim for fluency and a rhythmically flowing arm movement. Don't dip the wrist too far – the thumb still needs to play on its corner. Any occasional unevenness can be corrected by attentive listening. 'Tango': Drop more energetically into the phrases that begin *forte* – avoid pressing hard with the fingers. Revise 'Jellyfish jumps' for the *staccato* chords (Level 1, p. 17).
- **RP** Alexander Reinagle: 'Minuet' (Level 1, p. 38)
  Joseph Haydn: 'Zingarese' from Level 3, p. 31
  Walter Carroll: 'Dwarfs of the Mist'
  Friedrich Burgmüller: 'Arabesque' Op. 100 No. 2
  Christian Traugott Brunner: Rondoletto (in *The Joy of Classics* by Denes Agay)
  Dmitri Kabalevsky: 'Galop (Hopping)' Op. 39, No. 18
  Carl Maria von Weber: Scherzo in A minor

Page 9 — Elegant endings

- **R** Floating off (Level 1, p. 36); Tumbling fingers (p. 6).
- **LO** To encourage students to listen attentively to the ends of phrases and play them sensitively.
- **TT** Compare these elegant endings with more abrupt endings, such as in Schumann's 'Soldier's March'.
- **RP** Aaron Burrows: 'A Journey Through the Snow' (Primer A, p. 38), 'A Sad Story' (Primer B, p. 35), 'Whimsy' (Level 2, p. 22)
  Pachelbel's Canon (Level 1, p. 10)
  Daniel Steibelt: Adagio in A minor
  Carl Reinecke: 'Elegy' Op. 183 No. 2

Page 11 — Large parachutes

- **R** Parachute touch (Level 1, p. 7–12); The Parachute Touch (*The Complete Pianist*, pp. 87–90); The Splay (*The Complete Pianist*, pp. 209–212).

LO	To put the 'Parachute touch' into practice in larger intervals for a rich *cantabile* sound.
TT	Students with small hands should just practise fifths, sixths and (if comfortable) sevenths.

Play the chords in one flowing motion. The hand needs to drop, not press. Allow a subtle 'give' in the wrist on landing. The hand will naturally flatten slightly to play larger intervals, but avoid a high, tight wrist (a 'scary spider' position).

If the main knuckles (MCP joints) collapse, revise the strengthening exercises in Primer A (p. 15) and B (p. 12) and *The Complete Pianist* (pp. 510–513).

RP	Robert Schumann: 'Armes Waisenkind' Gerhard Schwertberger: 'Samba in Sixths' Juan Cabeza: 'Diversion 40' Cornelius Gurlitt: 'Morning Song' Op.140 No. 2

Page 14 Large jellyfish jumps

R	Jellyfish jumps (Level 1, p. 17).
LO	To play *staccato* chords without tension. To relax the hand between chords.
TT	Avoid playing chords that are beyond the reach of the student's natural handspan. 'Little Waltz': Students with small hands can omit the middle C in bar 15.
RP	Cornelius Gurlitt: 'Morning Song' Op. 140 No. 2 Gerald Schwertberger: 'Samba in Sixths' Juan Cabeza: 'Diversion 40' Dmitri Kabalevsky: 'Toccatina' and 'Sonatina' from *30 Pieces for Children* Béla Bartók: Minuetto in C major.

Page 16 Accents – Jump LAND and Accented syncopation

R	Hop and drop (Primer A, p. 30)

To play accented notes with a relaxed drop of the arm, using gravity rather than pushing into the keys.

LO	At first give the student plenty of time to lift the hand quite high to give power and energy to the accented note. In faster pieces, there will be less time for an actual lift, but the feeling of energy will remain.
TT	The accent should reflect the character of the piece. A lively piece is more likely to call for heavier or more aggressive accents, like *sf*.

In 'Calypso' the hand will land more gently for the *tenuto*.

'Polka': as an alternative, play both G and A in the left hand in bars 3 and 7 with the thumb.

RP	Béla Bartók: 'Vigoroso' No. 21 from *For Children Book 1* Mikhail Glinka: 'Polka' (complete version) Robert Schumann: 'Wild Rider' Op. 68 No. 8

Page 19 Starting on a black note

R	Skipping-rope technique (Primer B, p. 28–33); Evenly curved fingers (*The Complete Pianist*, p. 83 and p. 114)
LO	To maintain a good hand position when playing pentascales and root position triads in B♭, E♭, A♭ and D♭. To develop good fingering and technique for scales starting on a black note.
TT	Move the whole hand forward to reach the black notes comfortably and keep the fingers evenly curved.
RP	Mike Springer: 'Winding River' from *Not Just Another Scale Book* (Book 1) Diane Hidy: 'Black Key Majors' from *Smart Scales* J.S. Bach: 'Menuet in B♭' from *Anna Magdalena Notebook* BWV Anh. II 118 Ludvig Schytte: No. 24 from *25 Melodious Studies* Op. 108

Page 21 **Melodic minor scales**

- **R** Two-octave scales (Level 1, p. 34); Harmonic minor scales (Level 2, p. 41); Expressive scales (Level 2, p. 36); Evenly curved fingers (*The Complete Pianist*, p. 83 and p. 114)
- **LO** To develop familiarity with the topography and fingering for melodic minor scales.
- **TT** Place the hand near enough to the black keys for all the fingers to stay evenly curved. Allow a student time to check the key signature, layout on the keyboard and the fingering before starting to play.

    The ergonomic left-hand fingering for G melodic minor achieves a much more even scale than the traditional fingering starting on 5. It is worth introducing this fingering from the beginning. See *The Art of Piano Fingering: a new approach to scales and arpeggios*, Penelope Roskell.

Page 24 **Upbeats**

- **LO** To create liveliness on the main beat through springing upward movements.
- **TT** The wrist initiates the movement, pushing the hand forward and up and causing the finger to press into the key. Start with a high, energetic springing action, then gradually minimise the movement.

Page 26 **Run-ups**

- **R** Upbeats (Level 3, p. 24)
- **LO** Extending upbeats to two, three or four notes.
- **RP** Leopold Mozart: 'Burlesque' (German Dance) from *Notebook for Wolfgang*
    Cornelius Gurlitt: 'The Little Rogue' Op. 117 No. 18
    Ivana Loudová: 'Sleeping Beauty' (Šípková Růženka) from *Pohádky na dobrou noc*

Page 30 **Two-octave arpeggios (left hand)**

- **R** One-octave arpeggios (Level 2, p. 44); Two-octave scales (Level 1, p. 34).
- **LO** To create flowing arpeggios, using the 'Skipping-rope technique'. The arm takes the thumb to its note in one coordinated movement.
- **TT** The bridge finger needs to soften to allow the thumb to pass under.

    Encourage the students to close the hand after each interval (see 'One-octave arpeggios', Level 2, p. 44).

    Avoid elbow swings ('chicken wings'). The elbow should hang loosely and the whole arm act as one flexible unit. See also *The Complete Pianist*, pp. 136–139.

    Arpeggios can also be practised in a $\frac{4}{4}$ rhythm to avoid accents.
- **RP** Walter Carroll: 'Nightfall' from *Forest Fantasies*

Page 31 **Left-hand arpeggio groups**

- **LO** To develop a muscle memory of the different arpeggio groups.
- **TT** Studying arpeggios, and their fingerings, in groups in this way reduces the amount of practice time required. Hand size will influence the choice between third and fourth finger.

Page 32 **Two-octave arpeggios (right hand)**

- **R** F is for fingering (Level 1, p. 30)
- **LO** To understand ergonomic fingerings, with the third or fourth finger playing the black note, and achieve more flowing arpeggios.
- **TT** Students quickly become accustomed to the ergonomic fingerings given here if introduced at elementary level and not confused with other fingerings. For more information see *The Art of Piano Fingering: a new approach to scales and arpeggios* by Penelope Roskell.
- **RP** Ludwig van Beethoven: 'Allemande' WoO 81 (bars 1–8)
    Ignatius Sancho: 'Trip to Dillington' from *12 Country Dances for the Year 1749*

Page 35 **Dynamics explorer**

- LO   To encourage students to explore a wide range of dynamics.
- TT   Aim for physical freedom and good quality of sound.

Page 37 **Pianissimo cantabile**

- R   Sound explorer (Level 2, p. 23); Dynamics explorer (Level 3, p. 35); *The Complete Pianist*, pp. 155–159.
- LO   To play *piano* and *pianissimo* with a *cantabile* sound.
- TT   Many pianists resist depressing the key fully, for fear of playing too loudly. Encourage the student to depress the key gently but firmly all the way to the keybed and to continue to walk along the keybed for the rest of the phrase.

Page 39 **Melody and accompaniment**

- R   Playing *legato* (Primer B, p. 13–15); *Legato-staccato* (Level 2, p. 27) now played with different dynamics in each hand; Pianissimo cantabile (Level 3, p. 37).
- LO   To introduce dynamic contrast between the hands and an awareness of balanced piano sound.
- TT   If a student finds it hard to play the right hand louder than the left at this stage, just encourage them to *sing* the melody (aloud, or inwardly). Students who do not feel comfortable singing can just listen for a more *cantabile* sound in the right hand to encourage an instinctive physical response.

  Students may find it helpful to play the right hand with 'elephant steps' (a *portato* touch) initially, so the arm supports the tone production.

  'Melody': Depending on the level of the student, you may choose to omit the notes placed in brackets.
- RP   Christian Köhler: Etude in F Op. 190 No. 27

Page 41 **Left-hand melodies**

- R   The elephant walk (Primer B, p. 11); Left-hand melodies (Level 2, p. 41)
- TT   At this level, the emphasis can still be more on aural training than on the physicality of playing. When the student listens attentively to the bass line, the body starts to respond intuitively to the demands of the imagination.
- RP   Cécile Chaminade: 'Aubade' from *Album des enfants* Second series
  Béla Bartók: 'I love him from afar', No. 2 from *For Children* Book 2
  Melanie Bonis: 'Douce amie' from *Album pour les tout-petits* Op. 103 (ABRSM Grade 3, 2025–2026)

Page 43 **Wide leaps**

- R   Rainbows, Over the hills (Primer A, pp. 8–9), Leaps and bounds (Level 1, pp. 43–44), UM cha cha waltz (Level 2, p. 31); *Legato* pedalling (Level 2, p. 49).
- LO   To move accurately and confidently around the keyboard with flowing movements. To help play securely pieces with leaps from memory.
- TT   Aim for freedom of movement initially – accuracy will improve as the arm develops a confident memory of distances.
- RP   Frederic Chopin: 'Waltz' B150 Op. Posth
  Vitalij Neugasimov: 'Waltz-Caprice' from *Piano Sketches*

Page 45 **Duplets and triplets**

- LO   To switch between duplets and triplets while keeping a steady pulse.
- TT   Lift the wrist slightly to lighten the second and third notes of each triplet.

| RP | Johann Wilhelm Haessler: 'Poco allegro', No. 2 from *50 Pieces for Beginners* Op. 38
William Duncombe: 'Gavot' from *First Book of Progressive Lessons*
Béla Bartók: 'Triplets', No. 75 from *Mikrokosmos* Vol. 3
Alexander Reinagle: No. 24 from *24 Short and Easy Pieces*

Page 47 Repeated notes

| R | Repeated notes (*The Complete Pianist*, p. 178)
| LO | To change fingers on repeated notes to give the music a sense of direction.
| TT | As in repeated chords, two or more notes are played within one impetus. This is different from a finger flick action in which the fingers curl under the palm; instead, the relaxed hand places each finger in position, setting up a circular wrist motion.
| RP | Ludvig Schytte: No. 10 and 11 from *25 Melodious Studies* Op. 108
Louis Streabbog: 'The Woodpecker'
Cornelius Gurlitt: 'The Tightrope Dancer' Op. 130 No. 17
Friedrich Burgmüller: 'The Chatterbox' Op. 100 No. 17
Béla Bartók: 'Ballad (The Highwayman)' from *For Children* Book 2 No. 35

Page 50 Repeated chords

| R | Jellyfish jumps (Level 1, p. 17); Large jellyfish jumps (Level 2, p. 3); *Staccato* chords (*The Complete Pianist*, p. 244); Repeated chords (*The Complete Pianist*, pp. 244–247); Throwing the hand (*The Complete Pianist*, pp. 253–261).
| LO | To play relaxed repeated chords, using the natural rebound of the hand on the keys.
| TT | 'The New Doll' focuses on a relaxed rebound in *staccato* chords. The accent in 'Celebration Dance' requires a quick 'throw' of the arm on to the first chord. The repeated chords are then played within the impetus of the first chord.
| RP | Pyotr Ilyich Tchaikovsky: 'The New Doll' (complete version)
Béla Bartók: 'Dance' (Slovakian Dance), No. 8 from *For Children* Vol. 2
Dmitry Kabalevsky: Valse in D minor Op. 39 No. 13
Louis Streabbog: 'Jack Frost' Op. 64 No. 3

Page 54 Mordents

| R | Tumbling fingers (Level 3, p. 54)
| LO | To keep the arm light and the finger and thumb action neat. To explore different fingerings.
| TT | A light hand is crucial for good ornament playing.

Avoid making an excessive downward wrist movement as the thumb is played.

'Grandmother's Minuet': omit the lower D in bar 4 in the right hand if necessary.

| RP | Louis Streabbog: 'Merry-go-round' Op. 64 No. 10
Franz Schubert: Waltz in A major D 365 No. 28

Page 56 Trills

| R | Mordents (Level 3, p. 54)
| LO | To play simple trills with ease and confidence.
| TT | Aim for an even, steady trill, rather than a long, fast trill.

The 2–3 trill is primarily a finger touch. For a 1–3 trill a slight rotation will relax the arm. Start slowly, then gradually let go of any thought of rotation and just let the fingers twiddle lightly. (This process was described by Matthay as 'rotational freedom'.)

'The Trickster': the left-hand articulation can be modified to suit the movement of the right arm, for instance, in two slurs per bar (measure).

RP	Ben Crosland: 'Water's Edge' from *Easy Beans* Vitalij Neugasimov: 'Lazy Bear' from *Piano Sketches* Book 1 Ludovico Einaudi: 'Divenire' Carl Reinecke: 'Little Chatterbox' from *Children's Piano Pieces* No. 32

Page 58 **Inverted mordents**

- R Mordents (Level 3, p. 54)
- LO To practise neat, light inverted mordents.
- TT Most students will find it easier initially to play the ornament detached from the preceding note. The slurs in the Menuet allow students to lift their hand slightly before each mordent and play it with freedom.
- RP Elisabeth Jacquet de la Guerre: Menuet in F

Page 59 **Relaxed hand and fingers**

- LO To avoid exerting unnecessary pressure on the keys after tone production ('keybedding'). To avoid tension in non-playing fingers.
- TT Keep an eye out for tense fingers, which can manifest either as keybedding or as fingers sticking up. This kind of tension can affect the wrist and even the whole arm.

    'Pinky stiffness' may be a compensatory reaction for weakness and lack of stability in the other fingers, especially the fourth finger. Check that the fourth finger is firmly stabilised on the key.

    Encourage students to relax the non-playing fingers very consciously initially. Eventually this process will become instinctive – they will learn to keep the hand relaxed and play calmly from the key surface, even at faster tempo.

Page 61 **Held notes and Resting thumb**

- R Relaxed hand and fingers (Level 3, p. 59).
- LO To introduce finger independence in simple part-playing; playing two voices in one hand without tension.
- TT Relax the hand and finger after playing the held note – do not press into the key.

    'I Danced With a Pig': when playing *forte*, a more energetic forearm rotation will naturally start to occur.
- RP Narcisa Freixas: 'L'Ocell' from *Children's Piano* Vol. 1
Heitor Villa-Lobos: 'Fly, Little Bird'

Page 64 **Legato thirds**

- R Landing on thirds (Level 1, p. 10); Broken thirds (Level 2, p. 40); Relaxed hand and fingers (Level 3, p. 59).
- LO To play well synchronised double thirds without tension.
- TT Revise 'Relaxed hand and fingers' before studying this chapter, to remind the student to keep non-playing fingers relaxed.

    The 'breathing wrist' during rests will remind the student to keep the wrist relaxed while playing. The fingers need to stay sufficiently firm to play the notes together.

    The arm should stay in line with the playing fingers. Swivel the wrist outwards slightly to support the third and fifth finger as they play.
- RP Juan Cabeza: 'Station No. 2' from *Piano Train Trips*
Walter Carroll: 'The Little Brook'
Johann Hässler: 'Menuetto' from *50 Pieces for Beginners* Op. 38, No. 19
Louis Streabbog: 'Bees in the Clover' Op. 64

Page 66　**Direct pedalling**

- **R**　*Legato* pedalling (Level 2, p. 49)
- **LO**　To understand and become familiar with the difference between *legato* pedalling (foot rises on the beat) and direct pedalling (foot depresses the pedal on the beat).
- **TT**　Checklist:

  Place the ball of the foot on the pedal.

  Pivot lightly from the ankle with a smooth neat movement.

  Keep the leg relaxed.